the 10 best
ways
to add value
to your home

Sally Coulthard

Harlow, England • London • New York • Boston • San Francisco • Toronto
Sydney • Tokyo • Singapore • Hong Kong • Seoul • Taipei • New Delhi
Cape Town • Madrid • Mexico City • Amsterdam • Munich • Paris • Milan

Pearson Education Limited
Edinburgh Gate
Harlow
Essex CM20 2JE
England

First published 2008

ISBN: 978-0-273-71624-2

Commissioning editors: Emma Shackleton & Rachael Stock
Project editor: Patricia Burgess
Text and cover design: Annette Peppis
Illustrations: Peter Whalley
Picture research: Julie Knight
Index: Kathie Gill
Production controller: Amanda Thomas

Printed and bound in China   GCC/01

The Publisher's policy is to use paper manufactured from sustainable forests.

Picture credits
p.6 ©Loupe Images/Christopher Drake; p.28 ©Bieke Claessens/Redcover.com; p.44 ©Loupe Images/ Debi Treloar; pp.56, 58 & 67 ©James Balston/arcblue.com; p.70 ©Keith Hunter/arcblue.com; p.86 ©Grant Govier/Redcover.com; p.98 ©Practical Pictures; p.102 ©Reto Guntli/Zapaimages. com/Redcover.com; p.112 ©Loupe Images/Chris Everard; p.116 ©Mark Williams/Redcover.com; p.126 ©Practical Pictures; p.130 ©Chris Tubbs/Redcover.com; p.136 ©James Balston/arcblue.com; p.140 ©Ken Hayden/Redcover.com; p.148 ©Peter Durant/arcblue.com; p.151 ©David George/Redcover. com; p.152 ©Peter Durant/arcblue.com

contents

introduction

It's a well-kept secret but most home improvements are actually a waste of money. While many of us are busy laminating our living room floors or installing uPVC windows, the reality is that we're missing out on the most valuable additions to our homes.

When asked which jobs would improve the value of their home, most home-owners ranked a new kitchen, bathroom and a conservatory as the top three must-haves. Ask the same question to estate agents and you get a very different answer.

So what's the truth? Our home is our biggest asset, so it's vital that we invest our money wisely.

Most of us either remortgage or take out a loan to carry out home improvements. With borrowing levels at an all-time high, and interest rates looking uncertain, it's imperative that we get the biggest bang for our buck. And that's where this book comes in. Forget what you think you know about home improvements. This is the definitive guide to adding value to your property.

Each chapter takes one of the 10 best money-spinners – loft conversions, extensions, basements, kitchens, bathrooms, period features, redecoration, conservatories, gardens and roof terraces, garages and parking – and breaks it down in more detail. At the end of the book there's also a section on no-cost ways to boost your home's appeal to buyers.

The housing market varies greatly around the UK, and this is the first book to tell you which home improvements add most value in your region. You might be surprised to discover, for example, that adding central heating to a house adds more value in Scotland and the northwest than it does in the warmer southern counties.

The 10 Best Ways to Add Value to Your Home also debunks the myth that all improvements are worthwhile. We look at some of the best ways to waste your cash, depending on where you live, and just how far you should go with your renovations. Is it always better to have open-plan living? Does every house need a second bathroom? Should I pay for a new drive? This book will tell you when to let rip and when to leave well alone.

Each chapter aims to do a number of things: to explain the pros and cons of a particular renovation; to give you an idea of costings and potential profit; to look at the rules and regulations; and to help you decide whether to DIY or call in the professionals.

Don't take our word for it

While most property experts would agree on the best ways to add value to your home, it's good to know that the figures are backed up by research. In fact, the idea for this book came about after reading two fascinating bits of financial fact-finding.

The first is an ongoing project by the Nationwide building society, called *What Adds Value?*, which takes a comprehensive look at the factors that affect house prices, including home improvements.

The second piece of research was carried out by the online bank Egg, who asked 2000 home-owners and 110 estate agents which house alterations they thought added most value. The answers were markedly different and showed that many of us were undertaking the wrong alterations and wasting our money. Here's a quick summary of what they discovered.

Home-owners versus estate agents

Estate agents know exactly what sells and what doesn't. And yet it's amazing how few of us consult their opinion before carrying out home improvements. If we did, we might just discover that the things that add the most value to our homes aren't what we thought.

The table below shows the improvements home-owners said they would carry out to increase the value of their property. Next to that is the list of recommendations from estate agents. Who's opinion would you trust if it were your house and your money?

Regional variations

The second surprise from all this research was that the best-value home improvements differ according to where you live. In the hustle and bustle of London and the southeast, for example, loft conversions tend to add the most value to your home. That's because these areas are densely populated and people crave more space, so

Home-owners' top 10 value-adding improvements	Estate agents' recommended top 10 improvements
1 New kitchen	1 Loft conversion
2 New bathroom	2 Add a room via extension
3 A conservatory	3 A conservatory
4 Redecorate living rooms and bedrooms	4 New windows
5 Add a room via extension	5 New kitchen
6 Loft conversion	6 New bathroom
7 Garden decking/patio	7 Redecorate living rooms and bedrooms
8 Resurface drive	8 Resurface drive
9 New windows	9 Recarpet house
10 Recarpet house	10 Garden decking/patio

adding an extra bedroom will push up your house price considerably. In rural East Anglia, however, where space is at less of a premium, conservatories

Top Tip

■ ■ ■ ■ ■ ■ ■ ■ ■ ■ ■ ■

Estate agents should be your first port of call when deciding which home improvement to undertake, as they will be able to tell you what the local market demands.

■ ■ ■ ■ ■ ■ ■ ■ ■ ■ ■ ■

with great views of the surrounding countryside add the most value instead. It's interesting that in many areas of the country decking represents a poor investment if you want to make a quick profit from property.

Factors beyond our control

Ever heard the saying, 'Give me the strength to change the things I can, the courage to accept the things I can't, and the wisdom to know the difference'?

One of the key things to bear in mind when it comes to home im-

Regional estate agents' improvement valuations

UK Region	Largest value gain	2nd largest value gain
London	Loft conversion	Extension
East Anglia	Conservatory	Loft conversion
Southeast	Loft conversion	Extension
Scotland	Extension	Loft conversion
Yorks & Humberside	Extension	Loft conversion
East Midlands	Conservatory	Extension
Southwest	Loft conversion	Extension
Wales	Loft conversion	Extension
North	Extension	Loft conversion
Northwest	Loft conversion	Extension
West Midlands	Extension	Conservatory

SOURCE: EGG

provements is that you can take things only so far. At the end of the day 'fixed factors' play a huge part in determining the value of your house. In other words, it's vital to choose your house wisely in the first place. It's also important to accept that there's a limit to how much any particular house can be worth, even with a whole host of improvements. This is known as its 'ceiling price'.

Before discussing the things we can change about our houses, it's important to take a quick peek at the things that are beyond our control – the five fixed factors.

3rd largest value gain	Worst value gain
Conservatory	Decking/patio
Extension	Recarpeting
Conservatory	Decking/patio
Conservatory	Decking/patio
Conservatory	Recarpeting
Loft conversion	Decking/patio
New windows	Decking/patio
Conservatory	Decking/patio
Conservatory	Decking/patio
Conservatory	Recarpeting
Loft conversion	Decking/patio

1 Location, location, location

As irritating and clichéd as this phrase may be, it's also, unfortunately, true. Regional economic performance plays a huge part in how much your house is worth. Take London, for example. As a capital city, it will always attract huge volumes of people looking for work. This, combined with the fact that there is a limited stock of housing to choose from, creates a high demand for properties. High demand equals high house prices.

In fact, even within a fairly buoyant economy, house prices can vary wildly across the UK. The biggest difference in 2008 is between London and Northern Ireland: as shown in the table overleaf, an average London property costs roughly double a house in Northern Ireland. This gap has been closing, however, with many regions showing much faster growth than the capital. It's unlikely that the provinces will ever overtake London entirely, but it's interesting to see the effect that factors such as teleworking and faster transport links can have in terms of our reliance on big cities.

2 Good neighbours

Living in a prosperous, well-kept neighbourhood will always add value

Relative regional house values

	Property price 2006	No. of properties per London property	Rank
Inner London	£250,000	1.0	1
Outer London	£227,606	1.1	2
Southeast	£200,122	1.2	3
Southwest	£189,497	1.3	4
West Midlands	£170,433	1.5	5
East Anglia	£166,891	1.5	6
Northwest	£167,900	1.5	7
Yorks & Humberside	£158,426	1.6	8
North	£156,053	1.6	9
East Midlands	£155,599	1.6	10
Wales	£149,245	1.7	11
Scotland	£136,846	1.8	12
Northern Ireland	£118,190	2.1	13

to your home. At its most extreme, the difference is staggering. London now has the second-highest cost of living in the world (topped only by Moscow), thanks to record City bonuses and an influx of international billionaires. To give you an idea of the contrast between UK regions, the most expensive properties in London now fetch more than £4000 per square foot, making box rooms in Belgravia and Knightsbridge more expensive than three-bedroom houses in parts of Scotland and northern England.

The quality of your neighbourhood can also be affected by how well your local council is performing. Factors directly affecting your street, such as refuse collection and crime, are the responsibility of your council. In areas where residents say they are happy with their local authority, houses command an average of 3 per cent more than in areas where residents are dissatisfied. Another 3 per cent can be added to or subtracted from your house value based on the cleanliness of the streets.

	Property price 2003	No. of properties per London property	Rank
Inner London	£200,000	1.0	1
Outer London	£166,006	1.2	2
Southeast	£137,757	1.5	3
Southwest	£124,603	1.6	4
West Midlands	£108,772	1.8	5
East Anglia	£107,976	1.9	6
Northwest	£95,243	2.1	9
Yorks & Humberside	£90,260	2.2	10
North	£85,213	2.3	11
East Midlands	£95,898	2.1	7
Wales	£85,153	2.3	12
Scotland	£92,456	2.2	9
Northern Ireland	£76,096	2.6	13

SOURCE: NATIONWIDE

So while the exact location of your house is something you can't change, you can certainly try improving a small part of it. Setting up a voluntary community scheme, establishing a Neighbourhood Watch group, campaigning for better council facilities, or even entering your neighbourhood for the Britain in Bloom competition are all great ways to give your borough a much-needed kick up the backside. The fact that you'll improve the value of your home is surely a welcome bonus.

3 Older and wiser

Another fixed factor is the age of your house. Britain is a nation of history lovers, and we do like our homes with a bit of character. At the time of writing, houses built between the 1940s and the late 1970s command the least value. By contrast, there's a significant premium for Victorian, Georgian and even older houses. In fact, the most valuable houses in the UK, comparatively, are those built in the first half of the seventeenth century, commanding a premium of around 30 per cent over similar sized post-war housing.

The prestige of owning a period property is something worth thinking about if you live in an old house. While you can't – indeed, mustn't – attempt to create a fake period interior (faux beams, plastic cornicing, fake fireplaces, etc.), there's a lot to be said for reinstating historic features, such as sash windows and panelled doors.

Many Victorian and Georgian houses were victims of 1970s' streamlining, in which period features were ripped out or boarded over to create a simple, sleek look. Replacing these with authentic salvaged pieces or well-made reproductions will certainly boost your home's appeal to buyers. Chapter 6 tells you more about this.

In the past, new builds have always been popular and attracted high prices. However, this trend seems to be changing. In the late 1980s a new-build home would have set you back around 25–30 per cent more than a similar pre-owned house. This premium has now plummeted to just 6 per cent. The reasons aren't entirely clear,

Property premium for year of construction

Medieval (1000–1500)	20%
Tudor (1500–1558)	31%
Elizabethan (1558–1603)	32%
Jacobean/Carolean/Cromwellian (1603–1660)	34%
Restoration/William & Mary/Queen Anne (1660–1714)	24%
Georgian/Regency/William (1714–1837)	18%
Victorian (1838–1901)	8%
Edwardian (1901–1919)	2%
End WWI to end WWII (1919–1944)	4%
Post-war (1945–1959)	
Sixties (1960–1969)	-2%
Seventies (1970–1979)	-3%
Eighties (1980–1989)	3%
Nineties (1990–1999)	8%
Present (2000–2008)	12%

SOURCE: NATIONWIDE

but it could be due to the fact that period homes are becoming more desirable, and changes in planning regulations mean that new builds are being squeezed on to smaller and smaller plots.

4 All by myself

Another fixed factor that you can't change is whether your house is detached or not. Detached properties have always carried a premium, and not surprisingly: no party walls or noisy neighbours to worry about.

What you might not know, however, is that of all the types of property available in the UK, detached bungalows are the most in demand. The reason behind this is possibly the fact that Britain has an ever-growing population of elderly people, and detached bungalows are perfect for those with mobility problems. With the amount of relatively well-off pensioners increasing year by year, it's no wonder that detached bungalows rarely fail to sell.

For the rest of us (in ascending order of value on a square footage basis) flats remain the least valuable type of property, and are followed by terraced houses, semi-detached houses, semi-detached bungalows and detached houses.

5 Stamp Duty thresholds

It's vital that you take into account Stamp Duty thresholds (the level of tax payable on a house sale) if you are planning any home improvements with a view to increasing the value of your house. Stamp Duty is applied at different rates according to the value of a property, so improvements might lift your home from one band to another. At the time of writing the thresholds for residential property are as follows:

Purchase price	Stamp Duty
Up to £125,000	0%
£125,001 – £250,000	1%
£250,001 – £500,000	3%
£500,001 or more	4%

The effect of Stamp Duty thresholds is that they discourage people from going from one price bracket to another, thereby putting a ceiling price on your property.

For example, say your house is worth £240,000. You decide to add a loft conversion, hoping it will add around £25,000 to the value of your property, taking it up to £265,000. Unfortunately, thanks to Stamp Duty, a buyer will pay 3 per cent tax instead of 1 per cent, as the house costs over £250,000. In real terms, therefore, your buyer will have to fork out £7950 (3 per cent of £265,000) in Stamp Duty instead of £2500 (1 per cent of £250,000).

As a result, many buyers simply won't go over Stamp Duty thresholds. If the value of your house is just underneath a threshold, make sure that any home improvements take its new value well over the threshold.

Leasehold versus freehold

Most people have freehold properties. This means that they own both the house and the land on which it sits, and are therefore entitled to make whatever alterations they like (within planning law).

Those who live in leasehold properties (which tend to be flats) have effectively bought the right to live in the property for a number of years. Once the lease expires, the ownership of the property returns to the landlord. A short lease – one with less than 40 years to run – puts off potential buyers, who worry about the property reverting to the landlord and leaving them with nothing to show for all their mortgage repayments. Similarly, there is not much point in adding value to a property (via loft extensions and

suchlike) if it is about to be taken out of your hands. However, if you extend your lease by a significant amount (90 years, for example), you'll add value and saleability to your leasehold property – a much better investment than major building works, which, incidentally, need your landlord's permission.

The legalities of extending your lease or turning a leasehold into a freehold (known as 'enfranchisement') are complicated, but recent changes in the law have helped. There are a number of organisations that can help you establish how much it will cost to extend or change your lease. To find out more contact the Leasehold Advisory Service (see page 187).

Whatever you do, don't let your lease expire before doing something about it. If the lease ends, you no longer own your property, and your landlord may not be obliged to give you a new lease. If the landlord does refuse to give you a new lease, you then revert to being a tenant and will have to pay the market rental rate for the property.

Your property's potential

It might seem a bit pointless to talk about the factors that you can't change about your house when all you want to do is read about things you *can* do. But there is a reason behind this. To know what adds value to your home, you first need to have a realistic picture of where it sits in the UK property market.

Some people go crazy with renovations, hoping to increase the house value way beyond what it's inherently worth. Know your home's limitations and you won't waste your money on unnecessary improvements. Having a good grasp of the effect of fixed factors also gives you a head start if you're planning to invest or develop houses for profit. To find out more about some of the fixed factors that might affect the value of your house, there are a number of good websites to visit.

Value forecasts

For investors and developers who want an in-depth look at house values, try Property Forecasts (see page 189), an online company that uses technical data to predict future house values. At the time of writing you can access 3–5-year forecasts of house prices for most postcode sectors and districts in England and Wales – pretty useful if you're planning to put your faith, and savings, into property.

Glossary

HIPs

Home information packs (HIPs) are now compulsory for anyone putting their house on the market. The pack must contain an assessment of how energy efficient your home is, as well as other legal documents, such as searches and evidence of title (right to ownership). Most estate agents will organise a HIP on your behalf. It's therefore very important to keep any documents relating to improvements that affect your home's energy rating, such as installing central heating, new windows or loft insulation. Always keep the paperwork and guarantees when you have building work done.

Area information

If you want to get a profile of your area, or are planning to buy in a particular place, a quick visit to Up My Street (see page 190) is well worth it. This very helpful website gives you specific information about your postcode, including average house prices, housing trends, demographics, local schools and crime rates. It can even tell you how well your local council is performing compared to the UK average in areas such as housing, health, recycling and refuse collection.

Environmental information

After the particularly wet summer of 2007, people are beginning to realise that location isn't just about having nice neighbours. Environmental risks, such as flooding, landfills, radon and air pollution, are all factors that affect the value of property. Visit the 'What's in My Backyard?' section on the government's Environment Agency website (see page 185) to find out more.

Don't even think about...

Before we get on to the 10 best ways to add value to your home, it's worth taking a minute to look at some absolute no-nos. According to a recent survey by Direct Line Home Insurance, home-owners in the UK will spend around £150 million on 'improvements' that actually *reduce* the value of their house.

Further research, carried out by the BBC, found that home-owners were making the same mistakes time and time again. Most of the following problems can be easily remedied,

but it's amazing how much value they potentially knock off your property. Here are 12 of the worst offenders:

■ **A grubby house.** Cleanliness may well be next to godliness when it comes to house value. A dirty home is not only off-putting to potential buyers, but it gives the impression that the house is uncared for and may have serious underlying problems. **Knocks off £500.**

■ **Garden ornaments.** Get rid of those garden gnomes; ditto for garden ponds and crazy paving. There's a fine line between quirky and plain odd. Don't risk alienating any potential buyers. **Knocks off £500.**

■ **Dead or dying pot plants.** For the sake of a few quid, it's worth replacing any plants that have seen better days. Dying plants suggest that you live in a poorly maintained, badly lit house. **Knocks off £500.**

■ **Bad lighting.** Light can instantly have an effect on your mood. It's no wonder that buyers like a home that feels light and airy. Gloomy lighting or dark curtains will make your home feel claustrophobic and depressing. **Knocks off £500.**

■ **Exuberant interiors.** You might love your lime green living room, but a neutral colour scheme is much easier to sell. Walls painted in bold or clashing colours might put off buyers who feel they have to redecorate. **Knocks off £1000.**

■ **Carpet in the kitchen or bathroom.** Gone are the days when shag pile enhanced a bathroom floor. Buyers want sleek, hygienic, washable floors, not a rotting carpet hiding all manner of nasties. **Knocks off £1300.**

■ **Overcrowding.** Stuffing your home with furniture and knick-knacks will give the illusion that it's smaller than it is. Have a ruddy good clear-out and reap the rewards. **Knocks off £2000.**

■ **Dodgy extensions and porches**. Ugly add-ons are bad news for prospective buyers, who will have to knock them down and rebuild. Their construction might also have compromised the structural integrity of the house. **Knocks off at least £2000.**

■ **Swirly carpets.** Patterned or brightly coloured carpets are a dated disaster. The buyer will want to replace the whole lot, and might reduce the asking price accordingly. However, don't be tempted to spend lots on replacement carpets because you won't recoup your costs. A cheap, neutral option will work well. **Knocks off £2500.**

■ **Suspect electrics.** Dirty or paint-spattered light switches and sockets give the impression that your electrical wiring is old, dangerous and needs replacing. **Knocks off £3000.**

■ **Stone cladding or pebbledash.** Dated and bad for brickwork, any form of render also suggests that your building has something to hide. **Knocks off £3000.**

■ **UPVC windows.** Totally inappropriate for period homes. No wonder that over 90 per cent of requests by owners of listed houses to put in uPVC windows are rejected. **Knocks off £10,000.**

Other spectacularly bad ideas include installing a sauna, swimming pool, cheap laminate flooring, tennis courts in the garden, botched DIY jobs, turning a bedroom into a bathroom, and coloured bathroom suites. There are, however, lots of exceptions to the rule, so let's take a closer look at the best uses of your time and cash.

Paperwork and planning

Before you get your hands dirty, you'll need to deal with the financial and planning implications of any home improvements. This section outlines all the areas you'll have to tackle to get your ideas off the drawing board.

Financing your home improvements

Few of us are lucky enough to have tens of thousands of pounds sitting in the bank, so what are the options when it comes to financing any building work?

Personal loan

If you have a good credit record, most banks will be more than happy to lend you money for home improvements. That's because, in the current market, banks see people with property as a relatively safe bet. The benefit of a personal loan is that it is simple and quick to arrange, unlike remortgaging, which can take weeks to complete. The downside is that personal loans tend to have higher interest rates than mortgages, so you'll pay back more in the short term.

0% credit card deal

You have to be so disciplined with this option that it's recommended only for people with a firm grip on their finances. The main benefit is that you can effectively borrow the money for free, as long as you pay it back in full before the real interest rate kicks in. On the other hand, it will pay only for certain services and retail items – how many builders do you know who take credit cards? Any cash advances that you take from the card are usually exempt from the zero per cent deal and subject to high interest charges.

Remortgage

Borrowing against the equity in your house is usually the cheapest way to access money. If you are planning significant home improvements, this is probably the safest and cheapest way to proceed. However, there are certain caveats. First, watch out for any arrangement fees that your mortgage company charges for increasing your borrowing. If the charges are high compared to the amount you want to borrow, it might be cheaper to get a personal loan. Second, remortgaging can take weeks if not months to arrange, especially if your lender is a small company. Consider getting an independent mortgage adviser to help you – they usually have plenty of contacts and short cuts up their sleeves.

Home improvement loan

This tends to have a better rate of interest than a personal loan because it is borrowed against the value of your home. Depending on your available income and the amount of equity in your property, you can usually lay your hands on between £5000 and £150,000. Be warned, however, that the length of time you have to repay the loan will be shorter than if you re-mortgage.

Talk to an Independent Financial Adviser (IFA) about all your options, making sure that he or she knows your financial situation, how quickly you want to repay the loan, and what the loan is for. See page 187 for helping finding an IFA in your area.

Planning permission and Building Regulations

In each chapter there's a detailed section on planning permission and the Building Regulations that apply to each home improvement. However, it's useful to have a brief run-through here of the general principles so that you know what you are dealing with.

Two areas of legislation apply to home improvements. One is the Town and Country Planning Act, and the other is Building Regulations. Whatever you plan to do to your home, it is *your responsibility* as the home-owner to check whether you need permission from your local authority. Ignorance of the rules is no defence if you are caught carrying out illegal work. Failure to comply with the rules may also lead to severe financial penalties or prosecution.

In brief, planning permission affects *what* you can do to your home, while Building Regulations affect *how* you do it.

Planning permission

The Town and Country Planning Act dictates what you can do to the appearance of your home from the outside and what use you can put your home to. Any changes to your house, such as adding an extension or dividing it into flats, would probably need planning permission. Unlike Building Regulations, which are exactly the same across the country, the Town and Country Planning Act is open to some interpretation by local authorities. This means that one local authority might have slightly different planning rules from another. Every local authority should have its own planning department, and they almost always publish a set of guidelines for people who want to make alterations to their home. Pick up a copy of these guidelines from your local planning department, or view them online at the council's website, before you consider making any changes to your home.

Some minor changes to your home are covered by what is called 'permitted development'. This means that they don't need planning permission to go ahead. It can be difficult to judge whether you need planning permission or not, so always talk to your local planning officer about any ideas you have. You can arrange a face-to-face meeting, or you might be asked to fill in a brief Development Enquiry form so that your idea can be assessed in more detail. This service is free.

After talking to your local planning officer you will have established whether you need permission or not. If you do, ask to be sent the relevant forms. Fill these in as comprehensively as possible, enclosing all the plans and supporting documents, along with the required fee (usually around £150). Your application will then be assessed by the planning committee at your local council, and a decision reached

Top Tip

If you don't want to apply for planning permission yourself, an architect can do this as part of the job. Alternatively, you can employ a chartered town planner, who offers a range of planning-related services, such as submission of planning applications and appeals against refusal of permission. Find a planning consultant near you at the Royal Town Planning Institute's website (see page 190).

within eight weeks. Don't start work before planning comes through. Some home-owners make changes and then apply for retrospective planning permission in the hope that it will be more likely to pass because it has already been built. Don't. This is a risky strategy that rarely pays off. Worse still, if permission is refused, you'll not only be required to return your home to its original state, but you could also face prosecution.

Planning permission summary

■ Make contact with your local planning officer at the town hall. This is just an initial conversation to establish whether you need planning permission or not.

■ Do the paperwork. If you do need planning permission, fill in the forms and send them back to the planning office with the required fee and documents.

■ Wait eight weeks. Within this time you should get a decision. Do not start work without one.

■ Act on the decision. If you get the go-ahead, the permission remains valid for five years. If you are refused permission, or don't hear within eight weeks, you can appeal to the planning inspectorate. Details of how to appeal can be found on the Planning Inspectorate website (see page 189) or from your local council.

Building Regulations

Unlike planning permission, Building Regulations are universally applied across the country. Their purpose is to ensure that building work is carried out to appropriate health and safety standards. The regulations cover various issues, including fire safety, structural supports, sound insulation, electrics and drainage.

Building Regulations apply to most significant home improvements, including alterations, extensions and conversions. They also apply to minor works, such as installing an additional bathroom, changing the drainage, or replacing windows. If you have any work of this kind done to your house, you must have Building Regulations approval, otherwise it can make it very difficult to sell or remortgage in the future.

Building Regulations are usually handled by the Building Control Department at your local council. As with planning permission, it's always best to give the relevant officer a quick call before you start work, to check what approval, if any, is required.

If you *do* need Building Regulations approval, you can obtain this in one of two ways.

1 Full Plans application

This is considered the more formal route. You need to send the Building Control Department two copies of the detailed construction and site plans, the submission form (available from Building Control) and the appropriate fee. A Building Control surveyor will check those plans, usually within two or three weeks, and contact you if there is any extra information needed, or if the plans do not comply with the Building Regulations. If so, you will then need to submit amended plans or additional information.

When the Building Control officer is satisfied that the work will meet Building Regulations, he will issue an Approval Notice. You will then have approved plans to give your builder, or to work from yourself.

The benefit of this approach is that the plans are approved before work even starts. This means they can be used both to price the job and to build from, which is very useful if you are unsure of how much the work is likely to cost. The Approval Notice is also often required by banks and building societies if you need to remortgage or take out a loan to cover the building work.

2 Building Notice

This is a quicker, more informal route. Using this method, you simply send in a location plan, the submission form and the fee. A Building Control surveyor will appraise the submission and, if happy, the Building Notice will be formally accepted. This form of submission is suited to simple jobs where you are unlikely to be asked for additional drawings or information. The downside of this approach is that there will be no approved plans to build or price from, nor will you get an Approval Notice. The benefit of this method, however, is that work can start straight away.

Cost-wise, the Full Plans method splits the fee into two instalments, the first being payable on receipt of the application, and the second following the first inspection by a Building Control surveyor. With the Building Notice method, the whole charge is payable at the time of giving the notice. Both methods cost the same, and the fee will depend on the size and nature of the work.

Completion Certificate

Whichever method you use to apply for Building Regulations, a Building Control surveyor will need to carry out inspections of the building work at various stages. Once the work is complete, a final inspection will be undertaken and, if the work complies with the regulations, a Completion Certificate will be issued. This certificate is a vital document, and without it any sale or remortgage of the property will be impossible. Keep it safe or, even better, give it to your solicitor for safe-keeping.

Competent Persons Schemes

These schemes were introduced by the government to allow tradesmen and contractors to self-certify that their work complies with the Building Regulations, as an alternative to submitting a Building Notice or Full Plans application. This means that for certain home improvements, such as installing central heating or rewiring, if you employ a builder or tradesman who belongs to one of the professional bodies listed on pages 183–90, you shouldn't have to go through the rigmarole of applying for Building Regulations approval yourself. You also get peace of mind that the contractor belongs to some sort of regulated body.

Some of the better-known organisations that represent tradesmen who self-certify that their work adheres to Building Regulations are listed at the back of this book (note that some bodies represent more than one trade). For a comprehensive list, visit the Competent Persons Schemes pages in the Building Regulations section of the Communities and Local Government website (see page 184).

DIY or get the professionals in?

Recent research from Halifax Home Insurance revealed that British homeowners spend over £670 million each year fixing badly done DIY home improvements. Many people find themselves out of pocket as DIY disasters often aren't covered by contents or buildings insurance. In fact, in the rush to add value to their home, many DIYers actually lower their house price through botched jobs and dangerous repairs. In addition, 200,000 Britons are admitted to hospital each year as a result of DIY accidents.

That said, getting in a tradesman will cost you. On average, it costs twice as much to get a job done by a professional as it does to do it yourself. Any reputable tradesmen will also be busy, so you might have to wait for them to be available.

So where's a good balance? As you'll read in the following chapters, if you are a competent DIYer, there's no reason why you shouldn't save money and tackle some of the home improvements yourself. Repainting, for example, is a very cost-effective job that most people can tackle themselves. The key is to know your limitations and always call in the professionals for jobs that need guarantees or certification, such as electrics, gas or structural work. In some cases, you might actually invalidate your home insurance by doing the work yourself.

You also need to be aware that potential buyers will expect a flawless finish to any home improvement jobs. Any buyers with a keen eye will spot a badly finished DIY job and drop their offer price so they can employ an expert to do the task properly. Be realistic about your skills with a paintbrush or screwdriver.

Getting an estimate/ quote

You need to have a good idea of what the job is going to cost before you commit. Be careful that you know the difference between an estimate and a quote.

■ An estimate is simply a rough approximation of costs and is not legally binding.

■ A quote confirms in writing how much the job will cost, how long it will take, what the work entails and whether the cost includes VAT. Ideally, a quote should also include a schedule of works, which breaks down what will happen at each stage of the build.

It's always a good idea to get three quotes before starting a job. You shouldn't necessarily go for the cheapest one: a suspiciously cheap quote probably means the builder will be cutting corners or using cheap materials. It's also a good idea to go for a qualified tradesman who is registered with a Competent Persons Scheme (see page 184).

Getting your home revalued

Once any building work is completed, it's a good idea to have your home revalued. The purpose of this is twofold: first, it reassures you that your home improvements have actually added the value that you hoped they would; second, it will reveal if you are still adequately insured for the rebuilding cost of your home.

Most buildings insurance policies are index-linked, which means that they rise automatically every year in line with the Retail Price Index (RPI). However, this doesn't take into account home improvements that add value. For example, you need to re-insure your home if you have changed it from a two-bedroom to a three-bedroom property. In fact, if you make any alterations, structural or other-wise, be sure to inform your insurance company.

You can also get your home re-valued for mortgage purposes. If the value has increased in relation to how much you initially borrowed, you might be able to get a better deal. For example, if you originally bought your house for £100,000 and needed to borrow £90,000 to pay for it, chanc-es are that your mortgage company would have charged you a higher rate of interest for such a high loan-to-value ratio of 90 per cent. If, after your home improvements, your house is now worth £200,000, that means your mortgage is only 50 per cent of the value of your house and you are probably entitled to a better rate of interest. You might also want to get your home revalued to release some equity. Talk to an IFA or your mort-gage lender about getting your home revalued.

loft conversions

If you ask estate agents which home improvements add the most value to a home, the answer is always the same – loft conversions and room extensions. In this chapter we look at why loft conversions represent such good value for money.

Loft conversions have five basic advantages:

- By extending upwards instead of outwards, you don't lose any garden.
- Loft conversions tend to be less disruptive than traditional extensions because the majority of the work is in the roof. Most builders will wait until everything else has been done before knocking through to build the new stairs, thereby keeping mess to a minimum.
- Loft conversions are quicker to build than extensions. You can add an extra room in as little as 6–8 weeks.
- You don't usually need planning permission.
- Loft conversions allow you more living space without the costly expense of moving house.

This last factor is especially important as the one-off costs of moving are becoming increasingly expensive. Solicitors' fees, estate agency fees, removal costs and now the controversial introduction of HIPs (Home Information Packs, see page 17) have sent moving costs sky high. That, combined with the fact that more than five out of every six home-buyers now pay Stamp Duty, makes buying and selling a costly process. No wonder that staying put and extending looks like an increasingly attractive option.

Move or build upwards?

The difference in cost between a three- and four-bedroom house is, on average, £30,000. Moving home now costs an average £9500, compared

---

Costs versus profit

Loft conversions add around 15–20 per cent to the value of your home. As long as the cost of your loft conversion doesn't exceed 15–20 per cent of the value of your house, you're in profit.

Example

If your house is worth £200,000, the maximum value you could add with a loft conversion is around £30,000–£40,000. A loft conversion usually costs between £15,000 and £30,000 (£17,500 is the national average), so it's important to keep your conversion well under the higher threshold.

with £3000 in 1996, which brings your total moving bill to almost £40,000. If you have extended your mortgage to afford the larger house, you will also have increased loan repayments for the foreseeable future. Compare this to the cost of a loft conversion (£15,000–£30,000) and it's easy to see why most people decide to stay in their home and build upwards.

Is it right for your house?

There are some crucial factors that will determine whether a loft conversion is suitable for you and your house:

How will it affect the 'feel' of the house?

Does your house need an extra bedroom or more living space? A house with four bedrooms but only one communal downstairs room will feel 'top heavy'. Would the loft conversion make a better bedroom or playroom? What about an office or extra bathroom instead?

Do you have enough bathrooms?

The best value seems to be gained when you upgrade a house from two bedrooms to three, or three bedrooms to four. Be aware, however, that buyers will expect a second bathroom if you have four bedrooms or more, so make sure you factor that into your planning.

Do you have too many bedrooms already?

In most cases, you should be aiming for a maximum of four or five bedrooms. Properties with more than five bedrooms attract only niche buyers, so might take longer to sell. There is such a thing as *overdevelopment*.

Do you live in the right area?

The value that a conversion adds depends on where your property is situated. A loft conversion in central London will add far more value than it would to a house in the middle of rural East Anglia (see page 10).

What will you do for storage space?

A loft conversion means that you'll gain a room but lose a storage area. Have you got alternative plans for all the personal belongings you've been storing in the attic?

Do you have bats in the loft?

Bats are protected by the law as an endangered species. It is illegal to kill or injure a bat, or damage access to a bat roost. Having bats in your roof does not mean building work cannot take place, but you will need to contact the Bat Conservation Trust (see page 183) for their advice before you proceed.

Is the roof space suitable?

Can you stand up in the middle of your loft? If so, there's a chance that your roof space is suitable for a loft conversion. Most loft conversion companies specify a minimum ridge height of 2.3 metres. If in doubt, consult your local planning officer, or talk to an architect.

Houses built pre-1960 are often easier to convert than modern homes because they have steeply pitched roofs constructed from individual rafters, leaving a clear space in the roof void. Those built later may have a shallower pitch (and therefore less head height), but the main problem with them stems from their having trussed rafters. These are more difficult and expensive to convert because cutting into the timber trusses makes the roof unstable (see below and opposite).

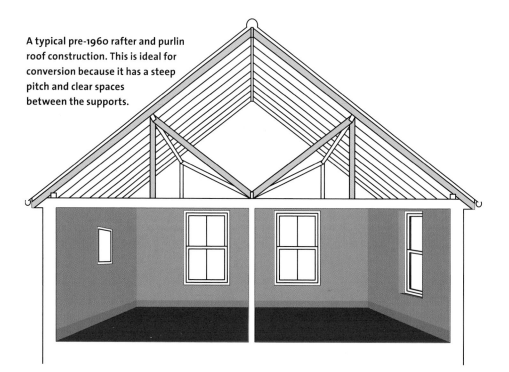

A typical pre-1960 rafter and purlin roof construction. This is ideal for conversion because it has a steep pitch and clear spaces between the supports.

Is it right for my family?

■ Loft conversions are ideal for growing families who don't want to face the upheaval of moving but need extra space.

■ Loft conversions are also ideal for families with older children, who prefer to have privacy and independence from everyone else.

■ People who work from home can enjoy the benefits of an office away from noisy living areas.

■ A loft conversion might not be the best solution for families with young babies or toddlers, who will not want to sleep on different storeys.

■ Domestic loft conversions tend to be unsuitable for people with mobility issues, such as the disabled or elderly.

Will I need planning permission?

The good news is that most loft conversions don't need planning permission because they fall inside your permitted development rights. You might need planning permission, however, if you:

■ live in a listed building;
■ live in a conservation area;
■ live in a flat or maisonette;
■ plan to add a dormer window;
■ plan to change the pitch, width or height of the roof.

Your local planning officer will be able to tell you more.

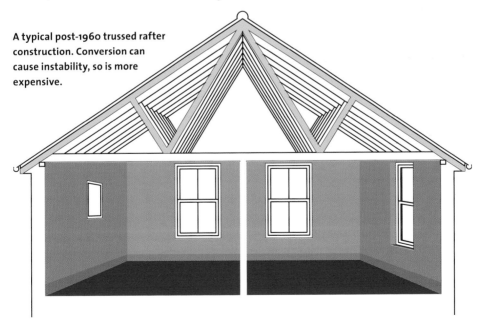

A typical post-1960 trussed rafter construction. Conversion can cause instability, so is more expensive.

Top Tip

■ ■

Keep an eye out for changes to the planning system. Current government proposals could result in all loft conversions needing to have planning permission. If you have been planning a loft conversion, it might be worth getting it done before the rules and regulations change.

■ ■

Glossary

Permitted development

You can make certain minor changes to your home without needing to apply for planning permission. This is called 'permitted development rights'. Some areas of the country are more restrictive than others about these rights. If you live in a Conservation Area, a National Park or an Area of Outstanding Natural Beauty, for example, you will need to apply for planning permission for certain types of work that do not need an application in other areas.

What about Building Regulations?

You might not need planning permission, but you will certainly need to comply with Building Regulations. These exist to protect the health and safety of people living in and around your home.

For loft conversions, the Building Regulations will strictly control factors such as:

■ Structural stability
■ Fire safety (including means of warning and escape, and stopping the spread of fire)
■ Weather resistance
■ Ventilation
■ Stairs
■ Thermal insulation
■ Sound insulation
■ Electrical safety
■ Drainage

If you are planning to turn your loft conversion into a habitable room, such as a bedroom or a home office, any building work must meet current Building Regulations. To do this you or your architect will need to make a Full Plans application or fill in a Building Notice application before any work starts (see page 24). Many conversion firms will provide this service for you.

A Building Control surveyor will want to come and look at your loft space to see if it is suitable for conversion. He might also want to inspect the build halfway through – in particular to look at any new floor and roof structures before they are boarded over. When the work is finished the Building Control surveyor will ask for a final visit to check that everything complies with the regulations, and only then will he issue a Completion Certificate.

The section of Building Regulations that relates to loft conversions has tightened up recently (especially in relation to fire safety), so it's important that you are up to date with the current legal requirements. For more information, talk to the Building Control officer at your local council, or check out the Building Regulation section of the government's Planning Portal website (see page 189).

Glossary

Planning permission and Building Regulations

People often confuse planning permission and Building Regulations approval. In simple terms, planning permission is about *whether* you are allowed to build or change a structure, while Building Regulations define *how* the new building must be constructed. Both are decided by the local authority.

Top Tip

■ ■ ■ ■ ■ ■ ■ ■ ■ ■ ■ ■ ■

Don't be tempted to carry out your loft conversion in secret. Without a Completion Certificate from your local Building Control officer, it can't be classed as habitable space when it comes to sell.

■ ■ ■ ■ ■ ■ ■ ■ ■ ■ ■ ■ ■

Loft conversions for storage

If you want to use your loft only for storage, Building Regulations still apply, but more loosely. Bear in mind, however, that increasing the non-habitable space in your house will add little or no value to your home.

Party Wall Agreements

As well as telling your local Building Control officer about your plans, it might be a good idea to talk to your immediate neighbours (those on either side) before any work starts. They will appreciate being kept in the picture, and therefore likely to be more forgiving of any disruption, but you are actually required by law to obtain a Party Wall Agreement if you live in a terraced or semi-detached property.

To serve a notice under the Party Wall Act, you must:

■ Write to your immediate neighbours at least two months before the intended start of the work. Give clear details of the work to be carried out.
■ Each neighbouring party should respond in writing, giving consent or registering dissent. If your neighbour does nothing within 14 days of receiving the notice, the effect is to put the notice into dispute.

Glossary

Party wall

A wall built on the boundary line of adjoining properties and shared by both owners (parties).

■ If the notice is put into dispute, a Party Wall surveyor can be called in to act as an intermediary and sort out any problems. Both sides will be represented, but the costs are usually borne by the side proposing the work.
■ No work may commence until all neighbouring parties have agreed in writing to the notice (or a revised notice).
■ Talk to your Building Control officer about drawing up a Party Wall Agreement or finding a Party Wall surveyor to act on your behalf. Party Wall surveyors can also be found in the Yellow Pages under 'Building Surveyors'.

Will I need my ceilings reinforced?

Your existing ceiling joists will almost certainly be inadequate for use as floor joists for the loft conversion. This isn't a problem, however, and in most instances it's easy to install new floor joists and supporting beams. It's best to talk to an architect or structural engineer, who will be able to provide calculations for any reinforcement needed.

Making best use of the space

Loft conversions aren't cheap, so it's vital you get the most for your money. Before work starts, make sure you've thought through how you'll use the space, what amenities you'll need up there (such as plumbing and lighting), and how you'll make the loft conversion feel like part of your home. Here are some pointers to get you started:

Stairs

If you plan to use the loft conversion for habitable space rather than storage, Building Regulations state that you need a permanent set of stairs of a suitable size. There are strict rules governing the pitch and width of staircases, as well as head clearance. If space is limited, there are special staircases called 'space savers', or you might want to consider a spiral staircase. Bear in mind, however, that these are less easy to negotiate than normal staircases. You'll also have to think about how you are going to get furniture up to the loft.

For ease and practicality you'll want to position the loft staircase running on from your existing stairs and landing. Otherwise, you'll have to reduce the amount of space in an existing first-floor room. Having the stairs as one continuous run also 'flows' better through the house, especially if the new staircase matches the old.

Storage

As mentioned earlier, what you gain with a loft conversion you somewhat lose in storage. It's therefore really important to make the most of any 'dead space' that you'll have. The area under the new staircase might provide an ideal place for a cupboard, while any awkward spaces in the loft (such as under the eaves) could be ideal places to install fitted cupboards and wardrobes. If you have dormer windows, consider a window seat with storage underneath, or a fitted waist-height cupboard.

Windows

Depending on the cost and scope of your loft conversion, you might have a choice about what kind of windows you have. The cheapest and simplest option is Velux windows or rooflights, which slot into the slope of the roof with minimum disruption.

Rooflight/Velux window

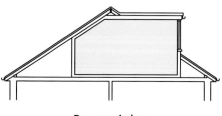

Dormer window

If you want more head height in your loft conversion, you might opt for dormer windows, which project out from your roof. These not only give you more available room, but will provide great views from the top of your house. The position of dormer windows is controlled by the planning authority – any developments have to be in keeping with the rest of your street – so you might be allowed dormers only on the back of your house and below the roofline. If you are lucky enough to have a gable end on your house, this could also be the perfect place for a window with a view.

Top Tip

■ ■ ■ ■ ■ ■ ■ ■ ■ ■ ■ ■

If the positioning of your windows is at all flexible, check that you are getting the best views for your money.

■ ■ ■ ■ ■ ■ ■ ■ ■ ■ ■ ■

En suite bathroom

No one likes to have to negotiate stairs in the middle of the night, especially when nature calls. If you are planning to use your loft conversion as a bedroom, try to make space for an en suite bathroom. Toby Cockcroft, a partner at Carter Jonas estate agents, explains why: 'Nine times out of 10, people use loft conversions as an additional bedroom. Whether it adds value depends on a number of factors. In my experience, creating a third bedroom in a two-bedroom terraced house usually creates the best return for your money. Large detached houses, on the other hand, which already have sufficient accommodation, might find the additional space doesn't add much, if any, value. In fact, too much undefined space can overwhelm a potential purchaser. If people specifically want to create additional bedrooms in the attic space, I always advise them to add a small en suite. This changes it from an occasional bedroom into a far more practical and saleable prospect.'

You'd be amazed how little space you actually need for a shower, basin and toilet. The drawings on this page show how much can be squeezed into a relatively small space, assuming you have enough head height. When it comes to fittings, you can also have fun shopping around for pint-sized suites. Ideal Standard has a range called Space, which is specifically designed for tiny rooms, while Micra makes a short-projection bathroom suite. Below are some possible solutions to creating en suite facilities in tight spaces.

Bedroom corner en suite

Minimum space required:
1600 x 1600 x 600 mm

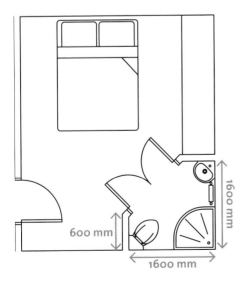

Standard bedroom en suite

Minimum space required:
2400 x 1100 mm

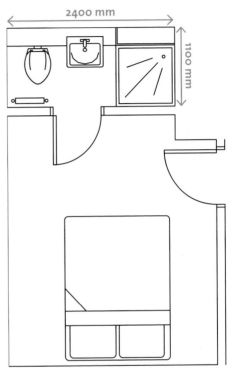

If space is really tight, you might want what is known as a cloakroom, with just a toilet and basin. Head height is also less of an issue if you don't need a shower. In fact, people often fit cloakrooms in spaces previously used only for storage, such as understairs cupboards or walk-in wardrobes.

Bedroom cloakroom

Minimum space required:

1200 x 1000 mm

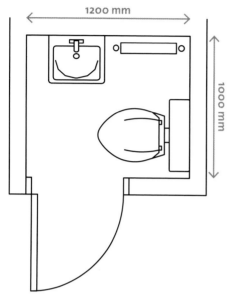

If you do want to include an en suite bathroom or cloakroom, you'll need to assess the water and waste services. One of the biggest challenges is getting toilet waste away from the loft. In a normal bathroom we rely on gravity to take toilet waste into the soil pipe and down into the drain. That is why soil pipes are often positioned on the outside of the house, right next to the bathroom. In a loft conversion it isn't always possible to connect the toilet straight to the existing soil pipe. That's where a 'macerator' comes in. It mashes up any toilet waste, then pumps it along a much smaller pipe that takes it out of the loft and into the existing soil pipe. The only downside is that you have to be really careful what you put down a macerating toilet – it can't process anything such as cotton wool, sanitary towels and tampons. A quick chat to a qualified plumber will help you establish what's feasible in your loft.

Electrics and heating

Have a really good think about where you are going to want light switches and sockets, as it's expensive to move electrics once you've plastered the room. Where will your bed go? Will you need sockets either side for bedside lamps? What about sockets for hairdryers and other appliances? Will you want a TV point or a telephone? Think about the lighting too. Low ceilings and pendant lampshades don't mix, so you might want to think about spotlights or table lamps on one main switch. If it's going to be a bedroom, would dimmer switches be useful? If you've got an en suite, you'll have to factor in ventilation, power showers and lighting.

If you want to put a radiator in the loft to run off your existing central heating system, check the position of your cold-water tank, and confirm with a plumber that your existing boiler can cope with the extra demand.

Make your loft feel part of your home

A loft conversion can easily feel like it's tacked on to the rest of the house, especially if you go for a cheap finish. You need to make it feel as though it's always been there, and the quickest way to do that is to bring in features from the rest of the house.

■ Can you echo the downstairs interior in the new loft? Keep with the same colours and floor finish.

■ Pick out details from other rooms, such as skirting boards or dado rails.

■ Make sure the windows match the rest of the house.

■ Are the doors and door furniture in keeping?

■ The staircase is particularly key to making your loft conversion feel part of the original house, so try to copy elements from the first-floor staircase, such as the handrail or newel post.

■ One of the most appealing things about loft conversions is their quirkiness. Make the most of odd angles, exposed beams and brickwork, and chimney-breasts.

It's worth saying, however, that you don't have to go overboard here. In Victorian and Georgian houses the attic was always the least decorated

Top Tip

Once the loft conversion is completed, you'll need to tell your home insurers. Adding an extra room to your property might result in a higher buildings insurance premium, but if you don't tell them, you could invalidate your policy.

part of the house, with much smaller fireplaces and less expensive fittings. In this case, make the loft feel like a pared-down version of the other floors in the house.

DIY or get the professionals in?

If you've weighed things up and are still tempted by the idea of a loft conversion, the next step is to decide whether you DIY or call in the professionals. Each has its pros and cons.

Competent DIYers should be able to tackle many of the elements of a loft conversion, including laying the new floors, putting plasterboard on the walls and ceilings, hanging doors, building stud-partition walls and installing the en suite bathroom. If you are having Velux windows, you might also feel up to installing those yourself, as most of the fitting can be done from inside the roof.

However, there are elements that you should get help with. All domestic electrical work done nowadays, apart from very minor works, has to conform with Building Regulations. To ensure this, you have either to employ someone who is registered with a Competent Persons Scheme (see page 25), or else do the work yourself and pay for the local council's Building Control officer to check your work. It's also strongly advisable that structural components, such as installing the staircase or strengthening the floor, should be carried out by a professional builder.

You can make huge cost savings by doing it yourself, but it could take you longer, causing more disruption to the home. It's also worth remembering that your own work won't be guaranteed, that a bad DIY job will actually devalue your home, and that you'll have to submit your own Building Regulations paperwork.

Hiring professionals? You have two options here: getting in a local builder or hiring a specialist loft conversion company. A reputable builder should be able to tackle most of the elements of a loft conversion, although he might have to subcontract specialist work, such as electrics and plumbing. If you decide to take this route, make sure you have a contract outlining costs and the nature of the job. The majority of problems occur when nothing is agreed on paper. Visit the Find a Builder website (see page 185) to download a free contract that can be used for any building project.

A one-stop loft conversion company, on the other hand, can handle everything from paperwork to plastering, but you'll pay for the privilege.

The benefits of getting in professionals are obvious. The job gets done quickly and efficiently, the work is fully guaranteed, and you don't have the hassle of all the red tape and paperwork (although check that this is the case before the work starts). It's a more expensive option than DIYing, so weigh up the total cost against how much value you think it will add to your house. Perhaps you could shave the budget by getting the builders to do most of the work, but decorating the loft yourself?

Loft conversion checklist

Before work starts

■ Check that your home is suitable for a loft conversion, e.g. does it have adequate roof height?

■ Plan what you'd like to include, e.g. bathroom, lighting, storage, etc.

■ Talk to an estate agent about potential value gain.

■ Get three quotes from appropriate tradesmen or contractors.

■ Do your cost/profit calculations.

■ Secure the finances.

■ Choose your specialist contractor (who will provide plans), or consult an architect, or draw up your own building plans.

■ Get planning permission and a Party Wall Agreement, if needed.

■ Obtain a Building Regulation Approval Notice, submit a Building Notice (or ensure tradesmen are part of a Competent Persons Scheme, if appropriate). Your contractor or architect might do this on your behalf.

■ Inform your home insurance company about the impending building work, especially if you are DIYing (any tradesmen or contractors should have their own public liability insurance, but double-check this).

During the build

■ Expect regular visits from the Building Control officer if you have applied for Building Regulations approval.

■ Keep a tight check on the budget.

After the project is completed

■ Expect a final inspection from the Building Control officer, and ask for a Completion Certificate to be issued.

■ Pay the tradesmen in full only when you are completely satisfied with the work. Ask for any guarantees to be issued.

■ Get an estate agent to revalue your home.

chapter 2

extensions

If you don't have the type of house that suits a loft conversion, or feel that you want a more substantial change to the layout, an extension is the obvious answer. You can transform the feel of a house by adding an extra room, but what are the specific advantages over a loft conversion?

Why extend?

- You can add functional downstairs rooms, such as kitchens, garages and utility rooms, rather than simply adding bedroom space.
- You can change the entire feel and flow of your home.
- You can construct a new space, not just convert an existing one. This allows you more flexibility and creative potential.
- You can build a room that allows you greater access to and enjoyment of your outside space.

On top of these advantages you also benefit by adding value and extra living space without incurring any of the costs of moving home. (See page 30 for more about the expense involved in moving.)

Is it right for my house?

There are some crucial factors that will determine whether an extension is suitable for you and your house.

Is the garden big enough?

Any extension will cut into the garden space. You'll need to decide if the outside space will balance with the inside space. A family-sized house needs a family-sized garden. A reduction in the garden area could actually devalue your property in spite of the extra floor space you've created.

Where will it go?

Where possible, alterations or extensions should be confined to the rear or side elevations. Front extensions never go down well with planners.

How will it affect the 'feel' of the house?

Again, you have to think about the proportions of the house. A huge downstairs living area with only a few bedrooms upstairs might feel 'bottom heavy'. As extensions tend to be on the ground floor only, they lend themselves to being functional or daytime rooms. Downstairs bedrooms and bathrooms are generally not as popular as utility rooms, kitchens and family areas. If you can build two storeys, however, it's always preferable to add an extra bedroom over the new living space.

Do I live in the right area?

Who lives in your neighbourhood? Extra bathrooms and large kitchens are usually good investments in family-orientated areas, while a garage in a heavily populated urban area will also add value. Regionally, extensions

Costs versus profit

Extensions add around 10–15 per cent to the value of your home. As long as the cost of your extension doesn't exceed 10–15 per cent of the value of your house, you're in profit.

Example

If your house is worth £200,000, this means that the maximum value you could add with an extension is around £20,000–£30,000. Depending on what you want, an extension can cost anything from £10,000 upwards; the simpler and more straightforward the work, the cheaper it is. Extensions on period homes tend to be more expensive if you need to match up existing bricks or stonework.

The best type of extension, and therefore the greatest source of added value, is one of the most desirable rooms, such as a family kitchen. If you can get permission, it's always good to build above the kitchen extension to add an extra bedroom at the same time. However, two-storey extensions are more expensive and less likely to be passed by the planning authorities.

An estimate of how much your single- or two-storey extension might cost is available from Estimators Online (see page 185). For a small fee, irrespective of the size of your proposed extension, they can give you a good approximation of costings. You should also remember to factor in the cost of decorating the extension, and any new furniture or fittings you want.

seem to add more value in the north and Scotland than in southern parts of the UK. This might be due to limited garden spaces in space-hungry places such as London and the south-east (see the table of regional valuations on pages 12–13).

Is my house suitable?

If you live in a listed building, there's a good chance you won't be able to add an extension; and if you do get permission, the costs could be prohibitively expensive. That doesn't mean all old houses aren't suitable. Owners of period homes must ensure that any extensions 'flow' from the original house – in other words, they should always match or complement the architectural style of the existing house. On the plus side, however, older houses often have more generous gardens, making it more likely that an extension would be acceptable to the planners.

Where will I park my car?

An extension should not compromise your provision for car parking, or cause road safety problems for you or your neighbours. Will you still be able to manoeuvre your car safely and easily if you can go ahead with the extension? The planners or your architect should pick up on this, but it's worth thinking about before you waste money getting plans drawn up.

Is it right for my family?

- Extensions are ideal for growing families who don't want to face the upheaval of moving but need extra space.
- People with mobility or disability issues can benefit greatly from increased downstairs space.
- More than one car in the family? A garage extension might well be the answer.

- Extensions can take longer to build than loft conversions, and be more disruptive. Is it the right time for your family to cope with building work? New babies, children swotting for exams, convalescing relatives and busy home-workers might not be able to cope with the chaos, however temporary. Consider renting for the duration of the works.

Will I need planning permission?

It depends. You must always check with the planning department before you consider an extension. You'll need to apply for planning permission if:

- your house is listed;
- more than half the area of land around your original house would be covered by the extension;
- you want to build an extension that would be nearer to any road than your original house, unless there would be at least 20 metres between your house and the highway. In this context the term 'road' also includes footpaths, bridleways and byways if they are public rights of way.

You will also need to apply for planning permission if your extension ex-

Glossary

Original house

In planning terms, 'original house' means the house as it was first built or as it stood on 1 July 1948 (if it was built before that date). Although you might not have built an extension to the house, a previous owner might have done so.

ceeds the prescribed limits on height or volume, as outlined below.

Height limits for extensions

■ You will need planning permission if the extension is higher than the highest part of the roof of the original house.
■ You will need planning permission if any part of the extension is more than 4 metres high and within 2 metres of the boundary of your property.

Volume limits for extensions

■ For a terraced house, or any house in a Conservation Area, a National Park, or an Area of Outstanding Natural Beauty, if the volume of the original house would be increased by more than 10 per cent or 50 cubic metres – whichever is the greater – you'll need planning permission.

■ For any other kind of house outside those areas, if the volume of the original house would be increased by more than 15 per cent or 70 cubic metres – whichever is the greater – you'll need planning permission.

Note: When calculating the volume of your house or an extension, it's the external walls rather than the internal ones that you should measure.

If you already have other buildings in your garden, these might be counted against your volume allowance. Always talk to your local planning officer first.

Top Tip
■ ■ ■ ■ ■ ■ ■ ■ ■ ■ ■

Calculating the volume of your house or extension isn't as straightforward as you'd think. Use the volume calculator on the government's Planning Portal website (see page 189), which gives you the answer in seconds, even if you have dormer windows, hipped roofs or other tricky-to-calculate features.

■ ■ ■ ■ ■ ■ ■ ■ ■ ■ ■

Permitted development summary

1 Extensions

Permitted up to 70 cubic metres or 15 per cent of the original detached or semi-detached house, or 50 cubic metres or 10 per cent of a terraced or end-of-terrace house, or a house in a Conservation Area.

Extension height **A** has to be a maximum of 4 metres if the distance to the boundary **B** is less than 2 metres. If **B** is more than 2 metres, extensions can be up to **C** in height.

2 Sheds and garages more than 5 metres from the house

Permitted if they are less than 3 metres high with a flat roof, or 4 metres with a ridge roof, as long as they do not project beyond any wall of the house facing a road, or cover more than 50 per cent of the garden area.

3 Garages within 5 metres of the house

These count as an extension.

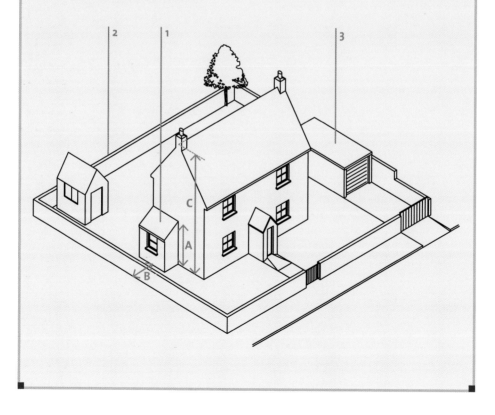

What about Building Regulations?

Regardless of planning permission, if you want to count your extension as habitable space, you'll need to comply with Building Regulations. In the case of extensions, Building Regulations are there to ensure that:

■ Existing and new foundations can support your planned extension.
■ Drainage arrangements are adequate for extra waste and rainwater.
■ Stairs and access are safe.
■ Ventilation, insulation and fire safety are satisfactory.
■ Any windows/doors fully satisfy the requirements for energy conservation and ventilation.
■ The extension is structurally sound.

As with loft conversions, you, your builder or your architect will need to make Full Plans or fill in a Building Notice application before any work starts. For more information, talk to

Glossary

Habitable room

A room in which people are likely to spend a considerable amount of time (i.e. not landings, hallways and toilets).

Top Tip

To make the planning application process as quick and painless as possible, it's important to provide clear, accurate drawings showing the existing buildings and what is proposed, any adjoining or neighbouring buildings, and notes to show existing and proposed materials. Photos are also a good idea.

the Building Control officer at your local council, or check out the Building Regulation section of the government's Planning Portal website (see page 189).

Garages and carports

If you want to create a garage extension, Building Regulations approval is required. However, Building Regulations do not apply to a carport provided it is open on at least two sides, and the floor area does not exceed 30 square metres. Detached garages are also exempt from Building Regulations provided:

- the floor area is less than 30 square metres;
- it is more than 1 metre from a boundary, or it is a just a single storey and constructed of wholly non-combustible material.

See pages 157 and 167 for more information.

Converting an existing conservatory

A relatively cheap and effective way of creating an extension is to convert an existing conservatory. There's a good chance that the foundations will be adequate for the conversion, and you'll already have walls and windows to work with. It's a challenge, but with a bit of careful thought, you can save yourselves thousands of pounds in builders' costs and materials. Replace the glazed roof with a solid roof, remove the wall between the conservatory and the existing house (inserting a rolled steel joist – RSJ), then plaster the walls, and your conservatory will feel much more like an extension of the original house. You may have to reduce the number of windows, but your Building Control officer can tell you more.

Converting an existing extension

You might have inherited someone else's extension with your house and decided that it's not enhancing your living space. A quick chat with an architect could produce some low-cost, high-return ideas that not only improve the feel of your home, but also add value. Replacing ugly windows or doors, changing the roof pitch or tiles, and rendering or painting unsightly external walls can all have a positive effect on the outside appeal of your home. Rethinking the internal living space is also crucial. Perhaps the extension isn't working as a bedroom – would it make a more effective kitchen or playroom instead?

Making best use of the space

An extension will undoubtedly change the feel and layout of your home, so it's vital to think carefully about how you'll use it. Here are some key issues worth considering.

Getting the balance right

As mentioned in the previous chapter, if you are planning to use your extension as a bedroom, make sure you have enough bathrooms to balance it out. The minimum ratio of bedrooms to bathrooms is 3:1, so a four- or five-bedroom house should have at least one family bathroom and a shower room. Buyers will like a downstairs cloakroom (i.e. toilet and basin), but ground-floor family bathrooms tend to be unpopular and impractical.

Avoiding corridors

One of the downsides to creating an extension can be that it makes the adjacent room feel like a 'through room'. In other words, you've gained a living room, but turned the old one into a corridor. Think about how you'll use the new layout and where the furniture will go. Instead of the extension being a separate room, would it be better to incorporate it into the existing room to create one large, useful living space?

Don't skimp on room size

Don't assume that any size of extension will add value to your home. There is a definite limit to how small you should go. It's also important not to try to squeeze too many rooms into your new extension – cramped spaces will make your house feel smaller, not bigger. The regulations are somewhat flexible, but as a general rule, a double bedroom should be no less than 10.2 square metres, a single bedroom 6.5 square metres and a dining room 9.5 square metres.

Big isn't beautiful

While mean proportions are disliked, it's a mistake to err in the other direction: very large extensions will be viewed unfavourably by planners and neighbours alike. The larger the extension, the greater its visual impact on the surroundings. Extensions should be subordinate to the original dwelling, and a size appropriate to the original house and locality. As a general rule, extensions should not add more than 20 per cent of the original floor space.

Be sympathetic to surrounding properties

Your extension will have an impact not only on the look of your house, but also on the entire street. To make your extension feel like part of the property and not just an afterthought, try to match the roofing material, guttering and exterior finish. If you have a period property, you might need to source reclaimed hand-made bricks or local building stone. Windows, doors and any other architectural details should also complement the house. Think about how the extension will sit with the rest of the houses in the street – are there any ways you can make it blend in?

Love thy neighbours

The planning authorities are careful that any plans for an extension will not harm your neighbours' quality of life or enjoyment of their garden. Extensions near property boundaries often cause problems for neighbours' outlook, privacy, access and natural light (see below). Note too that planners won't like extensions that have windows overlooking another dwelling's windows or private garden area to an unreasonable degree.

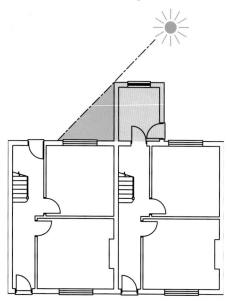

Carefully consider the position of an extension, as it might overshadow the windows and garden of a neighbouring property.

Top Tip

■ ■ ■ ■ ■ ■ ■ ■ ■ ■ ■ ■ ■

Make the most of soft landscaping. Trees, shrubs and grass can be used to soften the visual impact of your extension, pleasing both the neighbours and the planners.

■ ■ ■ ■ ■ ■ ■ ■ ■ ■ ■ ■ ■

DIY or get the professionals in?

There's absolutely no reason why an experienced DIYer shouldn't be able to tackle many elements of an extension, from planning to managing. If you want a very straightforward extension, and you don't need complicated drawings, you can work out what space you need and draw up the plans yourself. However, it's important that you have a firm grasp of Building Regulations before you start.

Much of the donkey work, such as digging the foundations and mixing concrete for footings, takes time and energy rather than skill, so even an inexperienced DIYer could handle this, saving a good chunk of the build cost.

In fact, if you're up to the job, the only tasks you shouldn't undertake are the electrics and windows. While you *can* fit the windows yourself, they'll need to be made by a FENSA-registered company (see page 186) or a contractor in a similar Competent Persons Scheme. Otherwise, Building Control will need to visit your house and check that any new glazing complies with current energy-saving and thermal-efficiency standards.

All domestic electrical work done nowadays, except very minor works, has to comply with Building Regulations. To ensure this you must either employ someone who is registered with a Competent Persons Scheme, such as NICEIC or NAPIT (see page 188), or else do the work yourself and pay for the local council's Building Control inspector to check your work. If you are going to do the building and structural work yourself, however, remember that it will be strictly monitored by Building Control. If you don't want it to look amateur, you must ensure that the finish is excellent.

If you live in a period property or suspect you'll need planning permission for your extension, it's advisable to consult an architect, even if it's just to help guide you through the red tape. An architect also knows how to get the most from your materials in terms of structure and aesthetics.

Perhaps you want something a bit avant-garde or modern? Maybe you need some advice about building an eco-friendly extension? If you want anything more than bog-standard, it's definitely worth getting an architect on board. If you want to be hands-off, most architects would also happily project-manage the build for you.

Builders will take on as little or as much of the project as you need. Many won't want to deal with the paperwork side of things, however, so it's worth clarifying who's going to be responsible for what. Builders tend to be good at the practical side of things, but don't expect them to be master architects too. If you want a specialised design, pay the money and get an architect on board.

Top Tip

If you live in a period property and need to source reclaimed materials, such as hand-made bricks or roof tiles, log on to Salvo (see page 190), the UK's most comprehensive salvage website.

Extension checklist

Before work starts

- Check that your home is suitable for an extension, e.g. how much garden will be left? Where will you park your car?
- Plan what you'd like to include, e.g. heating, plumbing facilities, etc.
- Talk to an estate agent about potential value gain.
- Get three quotes from appropriate tradesmen or contractors.
- Do your cost/profit calculations.
- Secure the finances.
- Choose your specialist contractor (who will provide plans), or consult an architect, or draw up your own building plans.
- Get planning permission and Listed Buildings Consent, if needed.
- Obtain a Building Regulation Approval Notice, submit a Building Notice (or, if appropriate, ensure tradesmen are part of a Competent Persons Scheme). Your contractor or architect might do this on your behalf.
- Inform your home insurance company about the impending building work, especially if you are DIYing (any tradesmen or contractors should have their own public liability insurance, but double-check this).

During the build

- Expect regular visits from the Building Control officer if you have applied for Building Regulations approval.
- Keep a tight check on the budget.

After the project is completed

- Expect a final inspection from the Building Control officer, and ask for a Completion Certificate to be issued.
- Pay the tradesmen in full only when you are completely satisfied with the work. Ask for any guarantees to be issued.
- Get an estate agent to revalue your home.
- If necessary, inform your home insurance company/mortgage provider that the work is complete and of the new value of your home.

basements

If you don't have space to extend upwards or outwards, another option could be to go downwards. Basement conversions are a popular way of adding extra rooms, especially kitchens, playrooms and utility areas. They don't come cheap, so why does it pay to have a room underground?

Why a basement?

■ You can add floor space without changing the outside appearance of your home.

■ Planners often limit the footprint and number of above-ground storeys of a building. Converting your basement gives you additional living space while meeting planning requirements.

■ Basements are often larger than loft spaces, giving you greater scope for living accommodation.

■ Converting the basement doesn't compromise your enjoyment of any garden space.

■ Research shows that houses with basements are up to 10 per cent more thermally efficient than houses of the same size entirely above ground.

■ Basements can be used for a huge variety of purposes – playrooms, home cinemas, music rooms, wine cellars, studios, kitchens, bathrooms and bedrooms.

■ Basements also can support rooms with unusually heavy loads such as garages, swimming pools and gyms.

Is it right for my house?

There are some crucial factors that will determine whether a basement is suitable for you and your house.

Is my basement suitable?

With modern waterproofing methods and structural engineering techniques it's possible to convert almost any basement into living accommodation. You can even create a basement from scratch – this is called a 'dig-out'. In practical terms, however, the latter option is very expensive (over £100,000) and would only be profitable if your home were located in a very exclusive area of the UK, such as Knightsbridge or Chelsea in London. The most realistic and practical basement conversions take place in houses that already have well-constructed basements. These tend to be in Georgian and Victorian terraced houses.

Top Tip

■ ■ ■ ■ ■ ■ ■ ■ ■ ■ ■ ■ ■

Want to know whether a basement conversion will make you a profit? Get a specialist basement conversion firm to assess feasibility and cost, then compare this to an estate agent's valuation of your home before and after the work.

■ ■ ■ ■ ■ ■ ■ ■ ■ ■ ■ ■ ■

Costs versus profit

Basement conversions can add 20–30 per cent to the value of your house. As long as the cost of your extension doesn't exceed 20–30 per cent of the current value of your house, you're in profit.

Example

Depending on the size of your home, the amount of excavation work required and various other factors, a full basement conversion for a typical Victorian terraced house would be around £75,000–£140,000. However, you can carry out a very simple basement conversion for as little as £20,000 if the existing roof height is adequate.

If your house is worth £200,000, the maximum value you could add with a basement is typically £40,000–£60,000, so it's probably not worth doing unless you can undertake a significant proportion of the work yourself. People in large houses, however, should get their money back and add value on top. As a very general rule, the minimum value of your home should be around £375,000–£400,000 to make the costings work.

What about head height?

If you want to do a budget basement conversion, the deciding factor will be head height (as this determines how much you'll have to excavate). You'll need a minimum of 2.4 metres for habitable space.

Do I live in the right area?

In rural and unpopulated parts of the UK, a basement conversion is probably a waste of money as space is at less of a premium. In expensive, highly populated cities with the right kind of terraced period properties – London, Bath, Manchester, Leeds, Edinburgh, Oxford, Bristol, York and so forth – there's a good chance you'll add significant value to your home.

How will it affect the 'feel' of the house?

While basement conversions are a good idea in many homes, the reality of living on so many different floors can be tricky. If you do go for a basement conversion, make sure you don't create just one room. If your basement is destined to be a kitchen, for example, make sure you'll have enough space to actually sit and enjoy your food, otherwise you'll be forever carrying plates and dishes up and down the stairs. If you want a bedroom in the basement, it's essential you fit en suite facilities into the plans, otherwise someone has a long journey to the nearest bathroom.

Glossary

Underpinning

The process of stabilising or increasing a building's foundations is known as underpinning. The soil beneath the existing foundation is excavated and replaced with strong foundation material, such as concrete.

Buildings need underpinning either when the existing foundations have moved or failed, or there has been the decision to add another storey either above or below ground level.

Is my house suitable?

If you live in a listed building, you might not be allowed to convert the basement, although period properties in general make excellent candidates for basement conversions as they tend to have generous underground space and timber-suspended floors. Basements can be excavated beneath modern solid-floored homes, but at a considerably higher cost due to the complexity of adding joists beneath the existing ground floor, as well as underpinning the whole basement.

What's the water level around your house?

The height of the water-table around your house affects the cost of a basement conversion. Anything is possible with enough damp-proof measures, but the costs may become prohibitively expensive. Your local water board or council should be able to tell you more. Failing that, any reputable basement conversion contractor should be able to establish the height of your water-table.

Is it right for my family?

■ Basement conversions are ideal for families who don't want the upheaval of moving, but need extra space.

■ Thanks to their generous size, basement conversions can often provide a totally self-contained living area, perfect for an au pair or granny annexe. If the basement has its own external access, you might even be able to earn extra income by renting it out.

■ Basement conversions, like loft conversions, tend to be less disruptive than extensions as most of the work takes place away from the living areas of your home. If it's possible, builders should be able to bring in and remove materials through the cellar light-well or coal-hole. There will be some noise and debris, however, so check that family members are happy with any potential daytime disruption. In terms of time, a small basement conversion can take as little as a month. Larger works can take up to six months.

■ People with mobility or disability issues might struggle to get the benefits from such a difficult-to-access living area.

■ Families with babies or very young children might not suit living in a home with so many levels and flights of stairs.

Will I need planning permission?

You'll be glad to know that most basement conversions don't need planning permission, unless you want to:

■ convert the cellar to a garage, separate flat or office, which counts as 'change of use';
■ change the external appearance of the building by adding a light-well; and/or
■ your building is listed;
■ you live in a conservation area.

As always, talk to your local planning officer before any work starts.

Glossary

Change of use

A change in the purpose or circumstance in which a building is used. For example, where the building:

■ is used as a dwelling, where previously it was not;
■ contains a flat, where previously it did not;
■ is used as a room for residential purposes, where previously it was not.

What about Building Regulations?

Whether or not you need planning permission for your basement conversion, you will need to comply with a number of Building Regulations. In the case of basements, these regulations cover such things as:

- Adequate fire escapes
- Ventilation
- Damp-proofing
- Electrical wiring
- Water and waste systems
- Structural underpinning and foundations
- New glazing

You, your builder or your architect will need to make Full Plans or fill in a Building Notice application before any work starts. For more information, talk to the Building Control officer at your local council, or check out the Building Regulation section of the government's Planning Portal website (see page 189).

What about the Party Wall?

Unless you have a detached property, you must also consider the Party Wall Act 1996. If you do not inform your neighbours about what you intend to do, they could stop the work. (See page 36 for more information on Party Wall notices.)

Making best use of the space

Basement conversions are a fabulous use of an otherwise underused space. The most successful are those that have tackled the problems inherent with basements, such as dampness and lack of light. Before you start, consider the following options to make sure you're getting the best use of your effort and hard-earned cash.

Natural light

Basements are naturally dark places, so it's important to introduce as much natural light as possible. If the basement is to be used for habitable purposes, you'll need an external door or opening window suitable for exit (Building Control will specify the size of window). Extra options for letting in natural light are discussed below.

- **Additional windows.** The highest part of some basement walls is actually above ground level, making it easy to add small windows around the top of the room.

■ **Light-wells.** These are short trenches dug along the side of the basement wall with a window installed. Many period terraced houses have these already, but it is also possible to install ones where none previously existed.

■ **French windows.** If your basement has access to the outside via a door, make the most of the opportunity and create a 'walk-out' basement with glass doors. It's also possible to create a walk-out basement from scratch, but the cost of removing a basement wall and reducing the outside ground level can be expensive.

■ **Light-tubes.** Also known as sun-pipes, these are a simple, inexpensive option. They funnel light from outside at ground level into the cellar through a reflective pipe (see below).

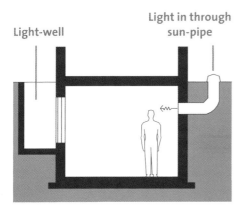

Light-well   **Light in through sun-pipe**

Section through basement

Artificial light

However much natural light you capture, it's always important to think about what happens after dark. Invest in practical and attractive lighting that includes task lighting, background lighting and focal point lighting. Dimmer switches are a quick way to add variety to the mix, while table lamps and uplighters add instant ambience. Don't underestimate the effect of firelight and candlelight to add to the picture, but forget fluorescent lighting, as it will make your basement feel stark and uninviting.

Ideal usage

Depending on its size and quality of light, you might want to think about the best use of the room. A naturally dark basement might make the perfect home cinema, while a light-filled converted cellar could provide an ideal studio space for art or music. Depending on its proximity to the road and traffic, check that the room is not too noisy to be a bedroom or nursery, or consider putting noisy teenagers or a games room in the basement if you want peace and quiet.

Sound insulation

Noise will filter both upwards from and downwards into a basement conversion, so make sure you allow for adequate sound-proofing. This should prevent disturbance from footfall above, and avoid upstairs annoyance from noisy activities below.

Storage

As with a loft conversion, go for as much concealed storage as you can create. Window seats and benches that double as storage are always a good option, while built-in cupboards and shelving will make the most of any tight corners.

Decoration

Reflect light back into your basement with strategically placed mirrors and light-coloured furnishings. If you want a light, bright space, keep window treatments to a minimum: use shutters, sheer fabrics and blinds rather than heavy curtains. Stick to paint colours that contain plenty of white, and keep any window ledges and rooms clutter-free. Paint the light-well white to reflect light back into the room, and think about light-coloured foliage outside to reduce the effect of staring at a blank wall. Your choice of flooring will also affect how light the room is. Carpets tend to absorb light, whereas floorboards with a high-gloss finish reflect it around the room.

DIY or get the professionals in?

Any job that involves disturbing the foundations of your house has to be undertaken with great care. You can, however, save money by doing some of the works yourself.

Either way, a basement conversion is a complex job, and the main elements should be undertaken by a specialist company. The jobs that you should always leave to the professionals include:

- Excavation
- Underpinning
- Drainage
- Damp-proofing

These tasks need to be done by professionals, not only because they involve large-scale machinery, structural supports and significant labour, but, more importantly, because if they fail, they cause the most damage to the home. By employing a specialist contractor you will have the benefit of work that is backed by a guarantee, and a certificate that shows it was carried out in accordance with strict Building Regulations. Any potential buyer would demand to have these two factors in place; without them your home becomes difficult to sell.

You can, however, tackle some parts of the job yourself. Once the major structural and waterproofing works are completed, there's no reason why a competent DIYer shouldn't be able to do the 'fit out' works, which include:

- Building stud walls
- Insulation
- Plastering
- Installing a floor
- Joinery
- Plumbing
- Decorations

To comply with Building Regulations, any electrical works in your basement need to be completed by a tradesman registered with a Competent Persons Scheme, or certified by Building Control. The installation of any central heating needs a registered CORGI (gas) or OFTEC (oil) installer.

Alternatively, you can get a reputable company that specialises in basement conversions to carry out the entire job from planning to painting. This option will cost you significantly more, but you have the assurance of a no-fuss, guaranteed job. Just make sure you are completely clear about who is responsible for any planning and Building Regulations paperwork.

Top Tip

■ ■ ■ ■ ■ ■ ■ ■ ■ ■ ■ ■ ■

Regardless of how much or how little of the work you want to do yourself, the Basement Information Centre (see page 183) can point you towards specialist contractors for drainage, tunnelling, waterproofing, underpinning and finishing work on basement conversions.

■ ■ ■ ■ ■ ■ ■ ■ ■ ■ ■ ■ ■

Basement conversion checklist

Before work starts

■ Check that your home is suitable for a basement conversion, e.g. does your space have adequate head height? Would a dig-out be cost-effective?

■ Plan what you'd like to include, e.g. a bathroom, light-well, etc.

■ Talk to an estate agent about potential value gain.

■ Get three quotes from appropriate tradesmen or contractors; check that they've taken into account factors such as the water-table.

■ Do your cost/profit calculations, then secure the finances.

■ Choose your specialist contractor (who will provide plans), or consult an architect, or draw up your own building plans. It's not recommended that amateurs tackle a basement conversion themselves.

■ Get planning permission, Listed Building Consent and a Party Wall Agreement, if needed.

■ Obtain a Building Regulation Approval Notice or submit a Building Notice. Your contractor or architect should do this on your behalf.

■ Inform your home insurance company about the impending building work, and ensure your contractor has his own public liability insurance.

During the build

■ Expect regular visits from the Building Control officer if you have applied for Building Regulations approval.

■ Keep a tight check on the budget.

After the project is completed

■ Expect a final inspection from the Building Control officer and ask for a Completion Certificate to be issued.

■ Pay the tradesmen in full only when you are completely satisfied with the work. Ask for any guarantees to be issued.

■ Get an estate agent to revalue your home.

■ If necessary, inform your home insurance company/mortgage provider that the work is complete and of the new value of your home.

kitchens

The kitchen has come to represent something more than a functional space. In the UK we have made the enjoyment of food a national pastime. Kitchens used to be purely practical places – often a no-go area for the man of the house. Times have changed, and although the kitchen is still considered primarily a female domain, men and children are increasingly coming in on the act. A well-equipped, stylish kitchen that encourages conviviality and interaction has become a must-have room in any house. Whether it's a rustic dream or a chef's paradise, an impressive kitchen can make or break a house sale. But why does a kitchen specifically add value over other home improvements?

Why a new kitchen?

- The kitchen is one of the most disruptive and costly rooms to replace. Most buyers don't want the hassle of fitting a new one.
- The kitchen is often the first room a buyer sees.
- The kitchen is the heart of the home – it sets the tone for the rest of the house.
- Reworking your kitchen space could give you more floor space and make the house feel larger.
- Kitchens sell the notion of a certain lifestyle; get it right and you make your home much more appealing.
- The kitchen is where we spend a large proportion of our time, so it's vital that the room is comfortable, clean and welcoming.
- When asked, female buyers still rate a good kitchen at the top of their

Costs versus profit

When asked, home-owners put kitchens as the best home improvement to add value. There are, in fact, better ways to add value – loft conversions, extensions and basement conversions – but these involve major structural work. A kitchen make-over is fairly straightforward, but still gives a home-owner the potential to add value. But by how much?

According to the online bank Smile, replacing a worn-out kitchen can increase the value of your home by up to 5 per cent. As long as the cost of your new kitchen doesn't exceed 5 per cent of the value of your house, you're in profit.

Example

If your house is worth £200,000, the maximum value you could add with a kitchen is £10,000.

Depending on the look you want, you can spend as little as £2000 or as much as £50,000 sprucing up your kitchen. On average, people spend £14,000 on their new kitchen, but to make this cost-effective, the house would have to be worth £280,000. It's important, therefore, to keep the amount you spend in proportion to the value of your home.

property wishlist. As women tend to have the final say when it comes to buying a family home, appeal to them, and you've got a better chance of a sale.

Is it right for my house?

There are some crucial factors that will determine whether a new kitchen is suitable for you and your house:

Is the kitchen scruffy?

Nothing kills a house sale quicker than a grimy, unkempt kitchen. It's time for a revamp if you have scratched or burnt worktops, cracked tiles, greasy units, missing handles, tatty floors, drawers that stick and old-fashioned appliances.

Are the kitchen units dated?

Anything earlier than 1990 will probably be looking tired by now. That said, original Victorian cupboards, sinks and shelves are real selling points, so don't be tempted to mess around with original period features. Aluminium kitchen units from the 1950s (made by English Rose or Boulton Paul) are also desirable. Even if you don't want to keep them, you can still sell them on to a specialist salvage dealer.

Does the kitchen fit the house?

If you've spent money on the rest of the house, don't allow your kitchen to let you down. It's also important that the style of the kitchen fits with the rest of your home. A country-style kitchen in a modern urban apartment, for example, will look distinctly out of place.

Is the kitchen big enough?

Narrow galley kitchens were once a common feature of mid-twentieth-century houses, but rarely impress twenty-first-century buyers. Most people want a kitchen large enough to cook in and eat in, so consider the feasibility of knocking through to an adjacent room to create a generous kitchen-diner. It's important, however, that by losing one reception room, you haven't compromised the layout of the house. Unless your home is completely open-plan, you'll still need a separate living area away from the kitchen.

Is my house suitable?

If you live in a listed building, there will be restrictions on what you can do to the inside, including remodelling the kitchen. Talk to your local council's Listed Buildings officer about any plans you have.

Glossary

Listed Building Consent

You *must* get Listed Building Consent from your local council if you want to alter a listed building in any way that would affect its character, *inside or out*. This can include removing fireplaces, painting over brickwork, stripping off plaster, removing beams or panelling, knocking down internal walls, making new doorways, and even moving small things, such as original cupboards and hooks.

Carrying out unauthorised changes to a listed building is a criminal offence, punishable by a large fine or a prison sentence. The local council will also make you pay for it to be put right.

Is it right for my family?

The type of kitchen you want will depend largely on three factors: your lifestyle, shopping behaviour, and how often you actually cook. It's important, therefore, to ask some key questions.

■ What kind of kitchen would suit your lifestyle? If you are a busy, working couple, would a low-maintenance, time-saving kitchen be best for you? Or do you want a kitchen that invites you to spend time cooking, eating and relaxing?

■ Do you socialise together as a family? Would your family benefit from a large, multi-functional communal space? Will people want to spend time in the kitchen, even when there's no cooking or eating going on?

■ Does much of your free time revolve around eating, drinking and cooking? If so, you will probably get great value from a convivial entertaining space.

■ Are you a serious cook? Do you spend a large amount of time in the kitchen? Do you need a more sophisticated kitchen than most?

■ Do you have young children? Think about their enjoyment and safety in a new kitchen. A child-friendly kitchen might include a few lower working areas, non-slip flooring and scratch-resistant surfaces.

■ How often do you go shopping? Do you need lots of space for food storage? Do you tend to buy fresh, frozen or packet food? This will dictate the kind of appliances and cupboard spaces you want.

■ Any kitchen refit will be disruptive: how will your family cope during the installation? There will be times when you might be without cooking facilities, hot water, and fridge/freezer. Can you make alternative arrangements during these periods?

Will I need planning permission?

You shouldn't need planning permission for a kitchen unless you are:

- moving walls;
- altering the drainage;
- changing the outside of your home to accommodate the new kitchen;
- living in a listed building;
- in a Conservation Area;
- making a separate home/flat by adding a new kitchen.

What about Building Regulations?

There are occasions when you might need Building Regulations approval. These include:

- Creating new drainage or altering an existing system.
- Provision for ventilation.
- If an existing room is being converted into a kitchen, you'll also need to meet requirements in respect of structural stability, electrical safety and fire safety.

If you are thinking of moving any gas pipes or fitting new gas appliances, these must be done by a CORGI (or similar) registered installer to comply with health and safety legislation. If you need any electrical work, make sure it is carried out by professionals registered with a Competent Persons Scheme (see page 25).

If in any doubt, talk to your local authority's Building Control department so that they can advise on any changes needed before work begins.

Making best use of the space

There's nothing better than a well-designed kitchen. Jobs take half the time, cleaning up is much easier, and the room feels inherently more enjoyable to use. Making the best use of space involves balancing your budget, your wishes and the practical restrictions of the room.

Layout

Traditionally, kitchen design is divided into four basic layouts, each of which is outlined overleaf.

Corridor kitchen

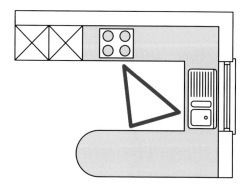

When space is really limited, and your kitchen is in effect a corridor, you have little choice about the placing of your appliances and units. They go on either side of the corridor, facing each other, with at least 120 cm between them to allow you to move around comfortably.

L-shaped kitchen

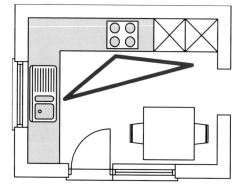

If you need to place the kitchen in a corner, the L-shaped layout is often employed to good effect. It also works when space is restricted.

U-shaped kitchen

Again, this is an effective use of minimal space as most units can be reached with little movement. It also works for a kitchen/diner, as the table can fit at the other end of the room. The space between the parallel sides of the U needs to be at least 120 cm.

Island kitchen

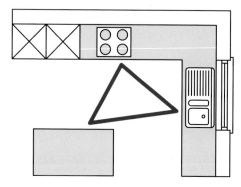

You need a generous room to accommodate a kitchen island, but a working area in the middle of the room does reduce the amount of toing and froing you'll need to do. An island also allows you to work in the kitchen without having your back to any other people in the room. You need to allow 120-cm gangways between the island and the units to permit comfortable movement.

Dynamic space

While layout is very important, so is a new concept dreamt up by the kitchen company Blum. Their idea of 'dynamic space' divides the kitchen into five different activity zones, the point being that keeping them separate reduces the amount of time a task takes and the distance you end up walking from one side of the room to another. The five different activity zones are:

■ Consumables – fresh, frozen and packet food.

■ Non-consumables – crockery, cutlery and glasses.

■ Cleaning – a 'wet zone', incorporating sink and dishwasher.

■ Preparation – the working area.

■ Cooking – the 'hot zone', including oven, hob, microwave and cooking utensils.

The zoned, colour-coded kitchen below shows how similar tasks are grouped together rather than spread randomly around. The surprising thing is that this layout really does reduce the amount of time you waste walking to and fro.

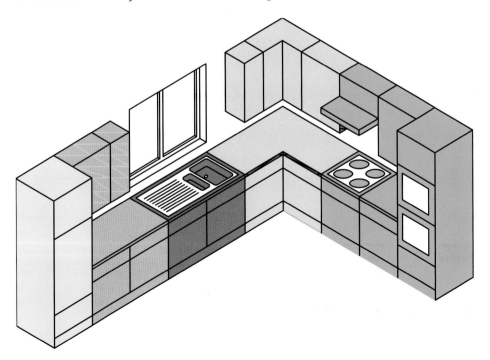

Kitchen storage

You have almost infinite options when it comes to kitchen storage. Along with all the space below the worktop, you'll have plenty of options for head-height storage, as well as clever little devices to make the most of every nook and cranny.

Below the worktop

The positioning of your oven, sink and fridge will dictate how much below-worktop storage you can have, but there's no reason you can't take advantage of some inventive ideas. Two-tier cutlery drawers, for example, have a sliding compartment on top of the one below, and get twice the quantity into the space, while deep drawers are perfect for storing heavy pots and pans. For full-height units, 'arena' wire drawers are ideal because they are see-through and accessible from all sides.

For tricky corner cupboards, carousels are a sensible option, but if the cupboard isn't deep enough, hinged doors can make an awkward space usable. Another handy storage solution that can be wheeled out when needed is a mobile butcher's block. This often incorporates rails, hooks and shelves, and tucks neatly under the worktop when not in use.

Not all below-worktop storage has to be in the form of cupboards. Wine racks are another option, as are wicker baskets for storing vegetables, and refrigerated under-counter drawers. Other innovations include warming drawers, which keep food warm, and bread drawers, which help baked goods stay fresh for longer (although these high-end additions tend to prove too costly for most budgets).

Finally, don't forget the wastebin. This is such an important part of the kitchen, yet is often an after-thought. Try to provide a generous under-counter area for a general bin, plus one or two others for any recycling you want to do.

Above the worktop

While it's not a good idea to store heavy items above the worktop, you can certainly utilise head-height space for some creative storage solutions. Traditional favourites, such as plate racks and spice cupboards, always look great in a country kitchen, while magnetic knife racks and utensil rails will add a professional touch to a modern space.

Above-the-worktop storage is also ideal for displaying favourite kitchen items, such as glassware and recipe books. Simple shelves are an easy option, but anything susceptible to grease and steam should be kept behind glass-fronted doors. And remember, the most often-used items need to be within closest reach.

On a final note about storage, some people say you can't have too much storage. You can. Don't store things for the sake of it. Have a careful think about what should stay and what can go. Are you ever really going to use that ice-cream maker or fondue set? If not, don't spend money on a cupboard when you could have extra floor space, a breakfast bar or room for another appliance.

Work surfaces

You have a number of different options for work surfaces, each with its relative merits. Your choice depends on your budget and the wear and tear your kitchen will receive.

Timber

An increasingly popular choice for worktops, wood looks fantastic and adds real warmth and character to a kitchen. If you source it from a sustainable supply (FSC certified, see page 186), you're also using an eco-friendly option. Wood is the only surface that doesn't damage sharp knives, hence its use for chopping boards, but that does mean it is prone to scratches and cuts. Wood will also burn easily if you leave a hot pan on it for too long. Price-wise, wood varies considerably, from relatively inexpensive beech to exclusive hardwood choices, such as mahogany and oak. To keep them looking good, wood surfaces need regular oiling, and might require the occasional sanding down to remove stubborn marks.

Granite

If quarried responsibly, granite is another great eco-friendly option, but it's usually chosen more for its looks and durability than its green credentials. Being 7 on the Mohs 1–10 scale of hardness, granite is virtually unscratchable. It's also cool to the touch, making it a popular choice for pastry chefs. On the downside, granite is a porous stone and will need resealing every year or two.

Quartz

Unlike granite, which is quarried in natural slabs, quartz worktops are actually a mixture of quartz, a binding polymer and natural pigments. This makes quartz worktops non-porous and therefore, ultra-hygienic. It also means they shouldn't need sealing. Unlike granite, quartz takes on the

Materials: pros and cons

	Pros	Cons

Timber	Looks fantastic
	Eco-friendly
	Doesn't damage sharp
	   knives
	Wide range of prices
		Marks/scratches easily
		Needs regular
		   maintenance

Granite	Looks fantastic Eco-friendly Durable Heat resistant Hard to scratch or mark Cool to the touch	Very expensive Needs resealing every one or two years
Quartz	Looks fantastic Eco-friendly Durable Heat resistant Doesn't need sealing Hard to scratch Not cold to touch	More expensive than granite

Laminate	Inexpensive
	Lots of colour/pattern
	   options
	Not cold to touch
	Stain resistant
		Cannot be used as a
		   cutting surface
		Easy to burn
		Difficult to repair

Stainless steel	Hygienic Heat resistant Flexible Stylish Resistant to corrosion Waterproof	Easily scratched and smudged Expensive Can look industrial

ambient room temperature – not good for making pastry, but much warmer to the touch. On the downside, quartz is about 10 per cent more expensive than granite.

Laminate

A cheaper option than either wood or stone, laminate worktops come in a wide variety of colours and finishes. On the plus side, they are ideal for budget kitchens and can handle a certain amount of wear and tear. On the downside, they damage easily and, once chipped or marked, are almost impossible to repair. They are also unsuitable for hot pans or using as a cutting surface. With improvements in technology, laminate is becoming more hardwearing, especially if you choose high-pressure laminate. Regardless of type, however, laminate is still an artificial product and isn't considered as eco-friendly as natural wood.

Stainless steel

Steel is the first choice in commercial and industrial kitchens because it is the only surface that can be bleached, making it both hygienic and practical. Stainless steel can also be manipulated into a variety of shapes, making it an option for all-in-one worktops,

Top Tip

If your laminate worktop has a tiny chip or scratch, it might be possible to fill it with an inexpensive Formica repair kit. The kits usually come with a range of tints and a mixing chart to help you match any colour worktop. Visit the Repair Products website (see page 189) for more information.

cupboards and splashbacks. While it is durable, waterproof, heatproof and resistant to corrosion, it is also easily scratched and expensive. In addition, it shows smudges very easily, although this can be reduced by using a textured stainless steel worktop.

Units

Most carcasses for kitchens are constructed using particleboard, whether it's MDF or chipboard. Not only is this cheaper than using solid timber, but it offers a more reliable framework on which to hang cupboard doors. Solid wood can warp with humidity and heat, whereas engineered timber will remain stable in most conditions. Cupboard doors, on the other hand, come in all shapes and sizes, with lots of different finishes. Whatever you choose, you have to weigh up carefully the various aesthetic and practical considerations. How much wear and tear will your kitchen have? Do you want surfaces that show fingermarks and smudges? Will your cupboards have to resist rowdy teenagers or careless lodgers?

Timber

If you buy a bespoke kitchen, the chances are that the doors will be made from solid wood. Clients like to see the results of hand-made joinery, and the aesthetics of real wood are hard to beat. Well-made, simple, solid wood doors will age beautifully and outlast a much more 'on-trend' kitchen. Wood itself comes in a wonderful variety of colours and patterns; there's also a huge variety of finishes to choose from, including waxes, colour washes and paint. Solid wood doors tend to be more expensive than 'fake wood', but there's no comparison in terms of finish and overall effect. Solid wood can also be refinished over and over again.

Wood veneer

This finish is a wafer-thin layer of real wood glued on to chipboard or a similar particleboard. Veneered cupboard doors are cheaper than solid wood, and give more uniformity in colour and pattern (if that's the effect you want). Despite their thinness, veneers are very durable and stain resistant, but once the top layer is worn down, dented or damaged, it can't be sanded or refinished.

Laminate

Home-owners love laminate cupboards because they are easy to keep clean. All they need is a quick wipe and they look as good as new. The downside is that laminate doors will eventually show signs of wear and tear, and at this point will need replacing as they cannot be refinished. Fake wood laminate also looks cheap, so use the material to its best advantage and go for bright, bold, modern statements.

Stainless steel

Units made of stainless steel can look really smart in a modern kitchen, but make sure you temper the clinical feel by combining them with natural materials and warm colours. A mix of wood cupboards and steel units always looks great.

Other materials

Lots of other materials are utilised to great effect in modern kitchens. Alongside the ones mentioned already, sandblasted glass, steel mesh, concrete, aluminium, cutting-edge ceramics, bamboo, Perspex and even cardboard can create practical and beautiful workspaces. Just remember to keep an eye on the budget – the more cutting edge the technology, the pricier it tends to be.

DIY or get the professionals in?

How much you do yourself depends on the complexity of the kitchen refit. A quick revamp is well within the realms of a competent DIYer, especially if you are leaving the plumbing, gas and electrics in the same place. The following quick fixes will spruce up a tired kitchen without needing to call in the professionals.

- Painting or replacing cupboard doors.
- Panelling with tongue and groove.
- Retiling and regrouting.
- Fitting new handles to doors and drawers.
- Painting or repapering the walls.
- Sanding, oiling or replacing worktops.
- Adding shelves, plate racks and other storage.
- Replacing the floor with wood, laminate or tiles.

For anything more ambitious, such as changing the units or layout of the kitchen, it might be prudent to talk to

Top Tip

If you're keen to design the layout yourself, IKEA has a downloadable kitchen planner that helps you to play around with the space and build a virtual kitchen. You can drag and drop kitchen units and appliances into layouts, view them in 3-D, and save them on your computer. Go to the IKEA website at ikea.com, click on the Interactive Kitchen Guide, and look for the link that allows you to 'Download the Planner'.

a kitchen company first. Many offer a free kitchen design service, which will help you to visualise the look of your new kitchen. Professional kitchen designers also have a fantastic knack of squeezing in storage, helping you to make the most of even the smallest room. You can arrange for a kitchen designer to come to your house or, if you prefer, you can take your own sketch plan with measurements to the store. Just remember to include all your electrical points, gas pipes and plumbing on the plan.

Once you've designed and chosen your kitchen, it's up to you whether you fit it yourself. Flat-pack kitchens are fairly straightforward to install, but sinks and built-in appliances can be tricky. If you're in any doubt, ask your kitchen supplier to recommend a fitter. You'll need to allow around £2000 to have a medium-sized kitchen fitted – and for that amount of money it's vital that your fitter belongs to a reputable trade association, such as the Guild of Master Craftsmen, the Federation of Master Builders, or the KBSA (see page 187).

As mentioned before, any changes to gas appliances or pipes, and any new electrical work, will need to be carried out by registered installers to comply with current regulations.

Kitchen checklist

Before work starts

■ Plan what you'd like to include in your new kitchen – worktops, cupboards, flooring, lighting, tiles, appliances, etc.

■ Talk to an estate agent about potential value gain.

■ Get three quotes from appropriate manufacturers, or shop around for a good, off-the-shelf deal.

■ Do your cost/profit calculations.

■ Secure the finances.

■ Obtain planning permission and/or Listed Buildings Consent if you are planning significant works.

■ Obtain a Building Regulation Approval Notice, submit a Building Notice, or ensure your tradesmen are part of a Competent Persons Scheme.

■ Inform your home insurance company about the impending building work, especially if you are DIYing (any tradesmen or contractors should have their own public liability insurance, but double-check this).

During the build

■ Expect regular visits from the Building Control officer if you have applied for Building Regulations approval.

■ Keep a tight check on the budget.

After the project is completed

■ Expect a final inspection from the Building Control officer, and ask for a Completion Certificate to be issued, if appropriate.

■ Pay the tradesmen in full only when you are completely satisfied with the work. Ask for any guarantees to be issued.

■ Get an estate agent to revalue your home.

■ If necessary, inform your home insurance company/mortgage provider that the work is complete, and of the new value of your home.

chapter 5

bathrooms

From the refreshing blast of a morning shower to a blissful candle-lit bath, the British have turned daily ablutions into a fine art. We absolutely *love* our bathrooms, and spend more on these tiny spaces than practically any other room in the house. Current figures show the average person will happily part with around £1500 for a DIY bathroom, or £3500 to get it done professionally. But is it money well spent? The short answer seems to be 'yes'. Most estate agents agree that a well-presented, newly fitted bathroom will not only increase the saleability of your property, but will also add value above and beyond your initial outlay. But what is it about a bathroom refurb that specifically adds value to a home, and is it worth having more than one?

Why a new bathroom?

■ Like kitchens, bathrooms appeal to women, who tend to hold the deciding vote when it comes to buying a house.

■ Of all the changes made to a house, revamping the bathroom causes the greatest inconvenience and potential for mess. Most buyers want pristine bathrooms that they won't have to do any work on.

■ Buyers have come to expect multiple bathrooms. Fifteen years ago, fewer than 10 per cent of homes had two or more bathrooms. Nowadays, it's well over 20 per cent. What's more, over three-quarters of all new-build homes have two or more bathrooms.

■ The wrong bathroom can be a real drawback if you want to get the best price for your property. Most buyers will be put off by a dated bathroom suite, grotty tiles and leaky fittings.

■ An old-fashioned downstairs family bathroom is particularly off-putting. People expect modern conveniences, even in period homes.

Is it right for my house?

Unless you live in a shoebox, the great news is that most homes can accommodate another bathroom or washing facility, even if it's just a down-stairs cloakroom. On pages 39–40 are diagrams showing the recommended minimum areas needed for en suite bathrooms and cloakrooms.

Where will it go?

Be clever about where you could fit a small bathroom suite – basement, loft, under the stairs, an unused porch, or the end of an existing bedroom. Even walk-in wardrobes and large cupboards can accommodate a compact loo and hand basin. Losing a bedroom to create an extra bathroom is rarely a good idea, as it radically reduces your home's ceiling price. Converting a bedroom into a bathroom may only pay off if your home is large, with at least five bedrooms and only one bathroom.

Is the floor structurally sound?

If you are planning to put a bath in your new bathroom, make sure the floor joists can take the extra weight. Cast-iron baths are particularly heavy.

Where's the plumbing?

If your pipes are in the wrong place, it can be prohibitively expensive to re-jig the layout. Save yourself hundreds of pounds by locating the new bathroom, especially any waste pipes, as

Costs versus profit

There's a difference in profit potential between simply replacing your old bathroom and adding a second bathroom.

Replacing the old bathroom

Revamping a tired family bathroom will certainly add buyer appeal to your home. On the average £200,000 house, a replacement bathroom will add up to 5 per cent on the value. In practice, that means you could add as much as £10,000. The average cost of replacing a bathroom is around £1500 to do it yourself, or £3500 to get it done professionally. As long as you don't go overboard on expensive fittings, it's easy to see why it's worthwhile.

Creating a second bathroom

A second bathroom will add even more value to your home – around 10 per cent. The figures differ regionally, however. In the east Midlands the average gain is about 7 per cent, while in London it can be around 15 per cent. In practice, that means an average £200,000 home would be worth an extra £14,000–£30,000 if you added a smart second bathroom, depending on where you live.

The cost of creating a second bathroom can differ greatly – from as little as £2000 to build a simple en suite, running into tens of thousands if you need to create a new extension. Keep the costs down, without compromising on quality and workmanship, and you're almost guaranteed to get a good return on your outlay.

There are provisos, however. The exact amount an extra bathroom will contribute depends greatly on the location and size of your home. It's easy to see, for example, that a one-bedroom flat wouldn't benefit from a second bathroom in the same way that a four-bedroom family house would. As a general rule, buyers expect at least one bathroom for every three bedrooms.

close to the existing system as possible. If you need to move the bathroom to the other side of the house, talk to a plumber about your options, including the possibility of installing a macerating pump.

How many bedrooms do you have?

As mentioned earlier, you probably won't make any money back if you add a second bathroom to a small one- or two-bedroom property, especially if it has limited living space. Houses with three or more bedrooms will definitely benefit from increased bathroom facilities, especially an en suite for the master bedroom.

Is your house listed?

If your home is listed, there's a good chance you'll struggle to get permission for any radical changes to the layout. That said, listed building officers appreciate the requirements of modern-day living. Have a quick chat with your local Listed Building officer – he or she might have some good suggestions. If you want to change the outside waste pipes, for example, you might have to use traditional cast iron rather than modern plastic. Equally, if you can create an en suite without knocking down any existing walls (i.e.

by adding a simple stud partition), that will have a greater chance of getting planning permission than more drastic works.

Have you added a basement or loft conversion?

No one wants to climb two flights of stairs to use a bathroom. If you've added a floor, you'll almost certainly have to add bathroom facilities to make the most of the new space.

Do we have space?

Play around with the proposed layout of your new bathroom. Get some masking tape and mark out the positions of the toilet, basin and any other sanitary ware on the floor. Don't forget to take doors, windows and radiators into account. Sizes vary greatly, but the average suite consists of a bath 1700 x 700 mm, washbasin 600 x 500 mm, bidet 370 x 550 mm, and toilet 500 x 700 mm. Make sure you have enough room to manoeuvre around these fittings. The suggested working areas around each unit are shown on the plan opposite.

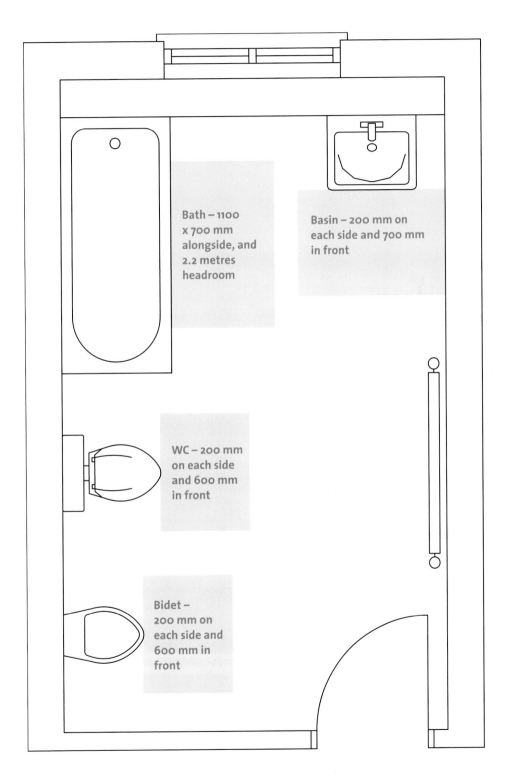

Bath – 1100
x 700 mm
alongside, and
2.2 metres
headroom

Basin – 200 mm on
each side and 700 mm
in front

WC – 200 mm
on each side
and 600 mm
in front

Bidet –
200 mm on
each side and
600 mm in
front

Top Tip

■ ■ ■ ■ ■ ■ ■ ■ ■ ■ ■ ■

Want to know what your new bathroom will look like in 3D? Take a look at one of the many online bathroom planners, such as Big in Bathrooms (see page 183), and build your dream suite from scratch.

■ ■ ■ ■ ■ ■ ■ ■ ■ ■ ■ ■

Is it right for my family?

■ Caring for an elderly or infirm relative? An accessible, downstairs bathroom will make life infinitely easier and more pleasant for both parties. It will also ease congestion on the existing family bathroom.

■ Is your family growing up? Older children and teenagers are notorious for hogging the bathroom. Could it be time to create a second bathroom or shower room to relieve the morning queues?

■ Planning to have guests? If you'd like to have a lodger, more friends to stay, or even open your home to Bed & Breakfast guests, it's definitely time to consider a second bathroom.

■ Putting your one and only bathroom out of use will make the house virtually uninhabitable. What alternative arrangements can you make?

Will I need planning permission?

Probably not. You shouldn't need planning permission to revamp your existing bathroom unless you live in a listed building or Conservation Area. If you plan to create a new bathroom as part of a house extension, you might require a planning application. Talk to your local planning department if you are in doubt.

What about Building Regulations?

If you are planning to make alterations to, or connections to, a drainage stack or an underground drain, you will need Building Regulations approval. All domestic electrical work, including supplies to power showers and macerating pumps, will have to conform with Building Regulations. Hire someone who is registered with a Competent Persons Scheme, such as BRE, British Standards Institution, ELECSA Ltd, NICEIC or NAPIT (see page 188). Water and electrics can be a deadly combination, so it's vital to get the work done by a professional. If the room is going to generate moisture (i.e. contain a bath or shower), you'll also need adequate ventilation. The position of any electrical lights is also dictated by Building Regulations (see page 95).

Making best use of the space

Throwing money at a bathroom will not necessarily make it a roaring success. There's a trick to bathroom renovation: get it right and there's the potential to add real value. Get it wrong and you are literally throwing your money down the drain. So what are potential buyers looking for? Here are just a few things to mull over before you spend a penny...

Make a splash

You don't have to compromise on style and functionality, even if your bathroom is tiny. Bathroom suites come in all shapes and sizes, including mini and slimline ranges from most of the major manufacturers. Property expert Sarah Beeny always recommends that however small your property, try to fit in a bath because you'll narrow your market if all you offer is a shower. With that in mind, bathroom manufacturers have come up with space-saving baths and corner baths that can fit on to walls just 1200 mm long. Back-to-the-wall toilet cisterns also maximise small spaces; as most of their plumbing is hidden (either behind stud walls or boxed in), they make the floor area seem larger and less cluttered. Another solution for a

Top Tip

There's no doubt that buyers like power showers, but check that your system is up to the job. Power showers and fast-flowing taps use a huge amount of water, which may not be feasible with your current set-up. Talk to a plumber about the possibility of installing a larger hot-water tank or an extra pump to cope with the demand. You also need to be aware that your energy bills will increase if your hot-water consumption goes up.

small space is to create a wet room. This accommodates a shower, sink and toilet without the need for a cumbersome and bulky shower enclosure. It's absolutely vital, however, that wet rooms are installed professionally and made completely watertight. This makes them expensive, so check with an estate agent that your outlay will be exceeded by any value you add to your home.

Simple suites

Buyers expect white. In fact, 95 per cent of bathroom furnishings sold in the UK are in various shades of white. Retro enthusiasts may insist that avocado bathroom suites are classics of the future, but don't be tempted to leave a dated suite where it is. When it comes to taps, you can't go wrong with chrome – simple, stylish and timeless. Brass taps can also look fantastic, but suit antique or reproduction suites better. Spend money where it matters. Cheap fittings feel light in the hand, so spend a little more on decent taps and shower fittings. If you need to save money somewhere, cut costs by choosing an inexpensive white suite from a DIY store and tarting it up with decent taps.

Ventilation and windows

If you are adding a bathroom from scratch, current Building Regulations require fan-assisted ventilation of all moisture-generating areas, such as showers or baths. There's a good reason for this. Condensation can cause damp walls, peeling wallpaper and rotting window frames. It can also encourage black mould and the growth of harmful bacteria. Another important reason for having good ventilation in a bathroom is to prevent the build-up of toxic fumes from cleaning and cosmetic products, as well as bad odours. An electrician will be able to calculate the type and size of extractor fan you need based on the volume of the room. Simply having an open window does not suffice – unless the room contains only a WC and washbasin. If you are refurbishing an existing bathroom, Building Regulations might not apply, but it's sensible to include a new ventilation system in your calculations anyway.

Don't forget to think about natural light. The most obvious solution is a frosted window, but what about having shutters, blinds or sheer fabric? Mirrors, glass walls and reflective surfaces can also bounce natural light around the room. In an en suite that has no wall space for a window consider the feasibility of having skylights or tube lights (see pages 38 and 65) to bring in natural light. Just make sure that any replacement windows comply with Building Regulations.

Lighting

Building Regulations dictate the positioning and type of any fittings. The rules are complex but, in brief, you are *never* allowed to use light fittings on leads in a bathroom, or to run a supply from an adjoining room (e.g. plug a table lamp into a bedroom socket and bring it into the bathroom – this is absolutely *lethal*). When you are planning where to put lights, you need to think about your bathroom having three different zones. Because of the different amounts of potential moisture in these areas, the types of light you can use differ. Light fittings in damp areas need to have a high ingress protection (IP) rating – in other words, they don't let in water vapour easily. For example, in Zone 1, which is right above the bath, you need a light fitting with a very high IP rating.

■ Zone 1 requires an IP rating of 68 or greater.

■ Zone 2 requires an IP rating of 44 or greater.

■ In Zone 3 there are no specific IP requirements, but you should talk to a qualified electrician to check that your lights meet current Building Regulations. Even in Zone 3, it's still recommended that you use an enclosed fitting.

■ Cloakrooms with hand basins but no shower or bath do not fall within the zoning regulations, but it's still

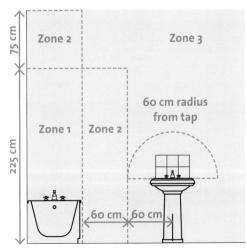
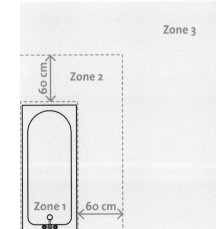

Aerial and side views of bathroom lighting zones.

important to check your ideas with an electrician.

With these rules in mind, flush-fitted halogen spotlights and mirrors with integral lights are two successful and safe options.

Privacy

Most home-buyers like their privacy, and nowhere is that more so than in the bathroom. We're a secretive lot and like to keep our bathroom activities to ourselves. We've already talked about frosted windows to spare our blushes, but don't forget that any glazed internal doors will also need to be obscured with opaque glass or clever curtains. There's also the noise issue. En suite bathrooms often suffer from being badly sound insulated, which can be embarrassing for all parties. You have a number of options available, from acoustic insulation to soundproof plasterboard (called Soundbloc). Your local builders' merchant will have more details. It might add a bit to your budget but you'll be thankful for it in the long run.

Open-plan baths and toilets? Great fun for a night in a swanky hotel, but not ideal for a domestic property: high-end or controversial bathroom designs can alienate potential buyers, even if *you* think they look fantastic.

Storage

Bathrooms often suffer from a lack of storage, especially when space is tight. Ironically, this is when good storage is most needed. Think about what you need to keep in your bathroom: towels, toiletries, dirty clothes, toilet paper, cleaning products and so forth. Certain items, such as medicines and razors, will need to be kept out of children's reach, so take that into account too. When space is at a premium, built-in storage or vanity units are a great idea, but you can also make the most of tiered trolleys (sometimes called 'bath carts'), wall cupboards and wicker baskets. Lots of companies make tallboys or free-standing shelves, which are ideal for stacking towels and toiletries. If you're really strapped for space, make the most of little-used areas: the back of the door, for example, could have a towel rack attached, and the shower tap could have a wire bottle and sponge rack suspended from it.

Decoration

Bathrooms, like kitchens, create a large amount of moisture. Your paint will need to work harder to retain its finish, so choose a product designed to withstand condensation. That doesn't mean, however, that you have to go for a dated, high-sheen finish. Companies such as Farrow & Ball produce washable, stain-resistant emulsion, with only a slightly increased sheen level. It also has the bonus of being one of the most environmentally friendly paints available. If you are particularly worried about condensation – above a shower cubicle, for example – you can buy anti-condensation paint, which actually insulates the wall and contains a fungicide to protect against mould growth (see International Paints, page 187). There is, however, no substitute for adequate ventilation.

As for colours, if you want your bathroom to appeal to the widest possible market, stick to neutral colours, such as creams, off-white and pale beiges. Light colours will also make the space feel larger and cleaner. It is possible to use strong colours in a bathroom, but take care not to make the space too individual to appeal to other buyers. Brilliant white can look cold and clinical, and may even make your bathroom suite look off-white, so always take the walls a shade darker than the bath and basin.

Flooring

Your bathroom floor will take a beating, so it's important to choose a hardwearing, water-resistant surface. It's also vital, however, that it's safe, slip resistant and easy to clean. You have a wide number of options: natural stone, such as slate or limestone, non-slip tiles, cork, wood and vinyl are all popular and practical. Polished granite and marble are simply too slippery, however, and carpet in a family bathroom is an absolute no-no.

Tiles

Go for simple designs and neutral shades. Most tiles are suitable for bathrooms, but bear in mind that those with a super shiny surface may be too slippery for use on the floor. Non-slip ceramic tiles are tough, resilient and waterproof – the perfect covering for bathroom walls and floors. They come in a multitude of colours and designs, including plain, patterned, glossy or matt, and even glass and metal versions for a hi-tech look. Mosaic tiles are always popular, and look great if used in varying shades of the same colour, or in oblong, brick-shaped tiles. DIYers, however, should note that mosaic tiles are notoriously tricky to lay, and might not be suitable for permanently wet areas, such as showers. Always check the manufacturer's recommendations.

Use what's there

If you are on a super-tight budget, a scruffy bathroom suite can be made to look (almost) as good as new with a bit of spit and polish. Limescale is easily removed with an appropriate cleaner, and most metal fittings will buff back to near original condition. Even if you have to get your bath re-enamelled and the taps replaced, you might still end up saving a small fortune. The toilet can be spruced up with a new seat, and a quick regrout or retile will finish the job nicely.

Antique fittings

For those of you lucky enough to own a period house it's always worth making the most of any original bathroom fittings, such as taps and handles. If you want to introduce them from scratch, think about reclaimed bathroom fittings for that extra touch of authenticity. Salvage yards are stuffed to the gills with antique sanitary ware and taps. From Victorian lavatories to stately roll-top baths, you'll be spoilt for choice. Just make sure you don't buy anything with a crack in it, and check that any plumbing has been reconditioned. A reputable reclamation yard will either restore the taps for you or be able to recommend a plumber who can.

DIY or get the professionals in?

Bathrooms done badly have the greatest potential to knock value off your home. Not only does botched DIY look terrible, but it's potentially deadly. A fifth of all fatal electrocutions happen in the bathroom, so it's vital that all the electrics comply with stringent modern regulations. To ensure this you have to employ someone who is registered with a Competent Persons Scheme (see page 25), or do the work yourself and pay for the local council's Building Control officer to check your work afterwards.

Plumbing is also an area that inexperienced DIYers should leave well alone. You might save money on labour, but are you up to the job? A recent Focus DIY survey revealed that 23 per cent of people said they would tackle refitting a toilet, and 26 per cent would replace a sink themselves. While this kind of home improvement chutzpah is to be commended, it's vital you don't get in over your head – burst pipes and leaky plumbing may not be covered by your home insurance if you were the person who fitted it. Always check with your policy provider first. Other jobs – painting, decorating and tiling – are well within the remit of the average DIYer. Just make sure you get a high-quality finish at the end.

If you are going for something more substantial, such as building an en suite bathroom or creating a wet room, it's vital you get in the professionals. You might not need the services of an architect, but you'll certainly need an experienced builder who can guide you through the maze of Building Regulations and structural issues. If you're keen to save money and are confident enough, you could suggest that you attempt the stud partitions, plaster-boarding and basic joinery.

Some schemes, such as creating a wet room, are best left well alone by DIYers. The floor needs to slope gently towards the waste in a gentle, consistent gradient, and must also be scrupulously watertight. In this case, it might be prudent to employ one company rather than try to project-manage several different tradesmen – this will ensure a clear chain of responsibility should anything go wrong.

Bathroom checklist

Before work starts

- Establish where your existing plumbing is and use this to help you work out where your new bathroom will go.
- Plan what you'd like to include, such as a shower, bidet and storage.
- Talk to an estate agent about potential value gain.
- Get three quotes from appropriate tradesmen or contractors.
- Do your cost/profit calculations, then secure the finances.
- Choose your specialist contractor (who will provide plans), or consult an architect, or draw up your own building plans.
- Get planning permission and Listed Building Consent, if needed.
- Obtain a Building Regulation Approval Notice, submit a Building Notice (or ensure your tradesmen are part of a Competent Persons Scheme, if appropriate). Your contractor or architect might do this on your behalf.
- Inform your home insurance company about the impending building work, especially if you are DIYing (any tradesmen or contractors should have their own public liability insurance, but double-check this).
- Arrange alternative washing and sanitary facilities, or your home will become uninhabitable.

During the build

- Expect regular visits from the Building Control officer if you have applied for Building Regulations approval.
- Keep a tight check on the budget.

After the project is completed

- Expect a final inspection from the Building Control officer and ask for a Completion Certificate to be issued, if needed.
- Pay the tradesmen in full only when you are completely satisfied with the work. Ask for any guarantees to be issued.
- Get an estate agent to revalue your home, then inform your insurance company/mortgage provider of the new value.

period features

As discussed in the introduction, period houses carry a premium over newer builds. In terms of value, the worst-performing properties are those built between the 1940s and the late 1970s. By contrast, Victorian, Georgian and even older houses command asking prices a healthy 10–30 per cent over similar-sized post-war housing.

New homes tend to suffer from the same problem as new cars – namely, depreciation in the early stages. Just as you lose thousands off the value of a car the minute you drive off the dealer's forecourt, so you knock 10–15 per cent off your sparkly new home the moment you move into it. In a sense, it's not surprising. The best bit about buying a new house is the fact that no one has lived there before you.

By contrast, the fact that lots of people have lived in your period home before you is part of its charm. The knocks and scrapes that a house acquires over a long period of time become like the patina on a piece of antique furniture: they make an old house completely unique. As a nation, we Brits are fascinated by our ancestors, and old houses are the nearest thing we've got to being in touch with our past.

But it's not good enough just to have an old house; people who want period properties want them because of their character, which in turn comes from original period features. Your home might look Victorian from the outside, but if it's a 1970s' nightmare on the inside, it simply won't realise its full market potential. That's why it's vital to replace missing period features. People who want a period home like to be surrounded by original elements – fireplaces, floorboards, cornicing, tiles, skirting boards, staircases, windows, stained glass, cupboards, screens and so forth. Original features set a period property in context. These features also tend to be made from expensive materials, often now unavailable or in short supply, such as mahogany, marble or pitch pine. It's no wonder that estate agents fall over themselves to point out period features. You don't see many house particulars that lovingly describe modern features in the same way.

Which period features should I replace?

You can't be expected to replace every period feature. Not only would it take an inordinately long time, but you'd blow your budget in a matter of days.

The first step is to do some detective work to find out what's missing. Look for evidence of old fixings, or holes or bumps in plasterwork. Doors, staircases and chimney-breasts covered with hardboard or plywood could be hiding original features. Lifting old carpets or lino can reveal original floorboards, tiles or stone floors. Ask your neighbours if they have any of the original features you can look at. Delve into books and magazines about the type of house you own – you'll soon get an idea of the right period features. In addition, the Bricks and Brass website (see page 183) has a great guide to working out what type of period fittings you need, or you can find out more about choosing and restoring original features in *The Reclaimers* by Sally Bevan (Hodder & Stoughton, 2005).

Costs versus profit

How much you should spend on replacing period features depends on a number of factors, including the age of your house. The Nationwide survey (cited on page 14) revealed that:

- Edwardian houses (1901–19) command a 2 per cent premium.
- Victorian houses (1838–1901) command an 8 per cent premium.
- Georgian/Regency/William houses (1714–1837) command an 18 per cent premium.
- Houses built between 1500 and 1714 command around a 30 per cent premium.

We can therefore use these figures as a rough indicator of what's appropriate to spend on replacing original features.

Example

Let's say you own a Victorian house that has none of its period features intact. If you replaced them, your house value would increase by 8 per cent. If your house is currently worth £200,000, that means you could, in theory, increase the sale price to £216,000. Similarly, if you're the owner of a Georgian house worth £200,000, you could raise that value by 18 per cent, or around £36,000. Choose your features wisely and there's certainly room for profit.

Top period features

Here's a quick run-through of what you should focus on and that buyers will be expecting to see in an old house.

Fireplaces

The most requested original feature, fireplaces represent the heart of the home. Open fires might not be practical for many people, but that doesn't seem to deter home-buyers from wanting original hearths, slip-tiles and fire-surrounds. If you choose to replace or open up a closed fireplace, you'll need help from a specialist, who can check on the ventilation and condition of your chimney. If you want to use an open fire, you'll also need to check that you don't live in a smoke-free area. Your local council can tell you this.

Cornicing and ceiling roses

Most people will be thrilled to see original mouldings on the walls and ceilings of a period home. Cornicing (which is the moulding at the top of the walls) and ceiling roses are often missing, but actually very easy to re-place. Don't be tempted to stick on naff plastic reproductions – interior mouldings were usually made of ei-ther plaster or timber.

Windows

Forget uPVC. Home-buyers will be ex-pecting original windows and glass, or high-quality reproductions at the very least. Windows are the eyes of the house, and the plastic ones can easily knock £10,000 off the average period property. Whether you're dealing with Georgian sash windows or stained-glass panels, it's vital to choose the right frame and style for the period.

Doors

It was the fashion in the 1970s to board over Victorian and Georgian internal doors. Removing hardboard facings

from these doors might reveal a nice surprise, but if the doors were long ago replaced, it's time to search for originals. Don't forget to source the right door furniture to match. Many buyers also like stripped pine doors, but bear in mind that exposed pine is not the original finish: the Victori-ans and Georgians regarded pine as a cheap material, and often painted it. An original front door will also make a stunning first impression.

Floorboards

Rather like our current fondness for stripped pine doors, our passion for bare floorboards would horrify our an-cestors. You can't get away from the fact, however, that old wooden floors look great and certainly add buyer ap-peal. It might be a job of simply lift-ing the carpet and lightly sanding the boards. If you need to replace missing or broken boards, reclaimed wood is easy to source from salvage yards or timber merchants. It's important, how-ever, that the rooms don't feel cold; you can soften the hard, echoey feel of wooden floors with plenty of rugs.

Tiles

Whether bathroom ceramics or an en-caustic tile hallway, original tiles are a joy. Don't worry if a few are cracked or

Top Tip

■ ■

Owners of period homes often find themselves coming to blows with listed building officers. If you want to make changes to a listed building, start the dialogue as early as possible. Have an informal chat with the listed building officer, describing what you hope to do and why, and invite suggestions. That way, you're more likely to reach an amicable agreement.

■ ■

discoloured – this all adds to their character. If large sections of patterned tiles are missing, however, these can be tricky to source. It might be easier to look for plain tiles of the right colours, or get a specialist company to source or manufacture replacements on your behalf. A search facility on the Bricks and Brass website (see page 183) enables you to find a period tile company near you.

Other popular period features, and those certainly worth highlighting if you have them, are original cupboards and shelves, Belfast sinks, light fittings and switches (just make sure they comply with modern standards), letter-boxes and other door furniture, panelling, early bathroom suites (especially roll-top baths), cast-iron radiators, wrought-iron metalwork (including fences and gates, shutters and screens), and staircases.

Where to source period features

The quickest way to get your hands on original period features is to head to a salvage yard, or shop for salvage online. But visiting a salvage yard isn't like popping down to your local IKEA. No two salvage yards are alike. Most appear to be chaotic, dirty and shambling (although you can guarantee that the salvage dealer knows exactly where everything is), but, more to the point, you never know what *you're* going to find. And that's part of the appeal of salvage hunting – there's nothing better than delving into a pile of junk only to discover an architectural gem sitting among the rubbish.

Hassle-free salvage

Whether you know what you're after, or just fancy a rummage around, it pays to arm yourself with a few top tips before you dash off to your local salvage yard. Follow these simple hints and you could save yourself a whole lot of hassle in the long run.

■ **Try to find salvage dealers who subscribe to the Salvo code.** Unfortunately, due to the high demand for period features and a few unscrupulous dealers, stolen antiques sometimes end up on the open market. Salvage dealers who have signed up to the Salvo code endeavour not to buy or sell items that have been stolen or taken from listed or protected buildings. Failing that, always get a receipt.

■ **Visit as many salvage yards as possible in your local area.** This will give you a sense of prices and value for money. Some yards tend to specialise in certain items, such as bricks or doors, while others offer a wider, more eclectic selection. If you have a specific object in mind, call the yard before you visit to see if they stock that kind of item.

■ **Do some research.** If you need to replace a historic feature, make sure you know exactly the style and date of the object you need. Each architectural period – Georgian, Victorian, Edwardian and so on – used very different proportions, styles and materials. Returning a period house to its former glory can be an expensive exercise. If you are strapped for cash, opt for authentic features that will have maximum impact and be the most conspicuous – doors, windows and fireplaces are obvious choices. If you're in doubt, use Judith Miller's excellent *Period Details Sourcebook* (Mitchell Beazley, 1987) as a starting point.

■ **Measure, measure and measure again.** Before you step foot out of the house make sure you have accurate measurements (in both metric and imperial) if you're buying something to fit a specific space. Include height, depth and width. And don't forget that your purchase will have to get into your house perhaps via narrow doorways or up stairs.

■ **Dress for it.** Salvage yards tend to be dusty and rusty, with much of the stuff outside, so don't turn up in your Sunday best. You'll need sturdy shoes, jeans and an old jumper, plus a strong pair of gloves if you plan to be doing any rummaging.

■ **Take a tape measure, notepad and pencil.** If you're trying to match an existing feature in the house, try to take along photos, drawings, fabric or wood samples – anything that will help you to make a sensible choice.

■ **Choose carefully.** Salvage yards tend not to give refunds if you change your mind. Some items might need restoration, so be very clear about what needs doing to an object before you buy it. If an object is sold as fully restored and working (a cast-iron radiator, for example), but is faulty when you get it home, you should be covered by the usual Trading Standards laws.

■ **Keep the kids at home**. As exciting as salvage yards can be, they don't make safe adventure playgrounds. Bricks, doors and all manner of heavy building materials are often stacked high alongside rusting railings and chipped ceramics – all accidents waiting to happen for a young child. In fact, many yards won't allow youngsters on site for this very reason.

■ **Talk to the salvage dealer.** Most yard-owners are experienced, savvy and very helpful; what they might lack in customer service they certainly make up for in knowledge when it comes to period features. Dealers are also a good source of contacts if you need an item restored or cleaned, and they might even suggest a different dealer if they can't help you with a specific item.

■ **Go armchair salvage hunting.** If you can't face rummaging in a real-life salvage yard, or you're looking for something quite specific, Salvo has an amazing online marketplace (see page 190). There are currently about 4000 items up for sale, from bygones to bridges and everything in between. At the time of writing the selection includes a complete Victorian shop front, Art Deco cinema seats, and a rare French Gothic Revival chimney-piece. You can search by region or by the type of item you're looking for. Or, if you want to locate a specific item, you can place an ad in their 'Wanted' section. You can also find reclamation on websites such as ebay.co.uk, or in the ads pages of local newspapers.

■ **Consider alternatives.** If you're struggling to find the right period feature, you might want to think about a reproduction. Reproductions tend to have a bad name, thanks to a large number of poor-quality imitations, but craftsmen-made replacements can be a good option if all else fails. Don't bother with mass-produced repros – they just won't have the same effect as the real deal, and most buyers will be able to tell the difference at a glance.

Will I need planning permission, Building Regulations or Listed Buildings Consent?

You shouldn't need planning permission unless:

- your period home is listed;
- you are planning to move walls or alter the outside of your home;
- you live in a conservation area.

Certain alterations, such as plumbing and electrics, will probably require Building Regulations approval, or need to be completed by a member of a Competent Persons Scheme. As always, talk to your local council if you have any questions.

If you do own a listed building, it's vital to talk to the conservation officer at the local Planning Department before you start work. It might seem odd that you need Listed Buildings Consent to replace period features,

Glossary

Listed buildings

When buildings are 'listed' they are placed on statutory lists of buildings of 'special architectural or historic interest'. These are compiled by the secretary of state for culture, media and sport, and are divided into three groups, according to their merit:

Grade I buildings are those of exceptional interest.

Grade II* buildings are particularly important and of more than special interest.

Grade II buildings are of special interest, warranting every effort to preserve them.

Most domestic listed buildings are Grade II. Contrary to popular belief, what you are permitted to do to a listed building is not affected by its grading – the same stringent rules apply to all.

but it's not as simple as that. The reason your house is listed is because it is in some way historically important – a physical relic that can reveal clues about the past. Building historians like to be able to 'read' an old building to establish what has happened to it over the course of its existence. Putting 'new' period features in a listed building, however well intentioned, might create a false history for it. The local conservation officer will have to be convinced that your proposals match the building exactly, otherwise it could be difficult to get planning permission.

DIY or get the professionals in?

With period buildings It's difficult to say whether you should DIY or get a professional in because each job will be so different. Replacing a period feature could be as simple as fitting a doorknob or as complex as repairing a stained-glass window. If you plan to do it yourself, here are five golden rules to help get you started:

1   **If it ain't broke, don't fix it.** More damage can be done in over-restoring a property than under-restoring it. If an architectural feature is broken or damaged, always try to repair it rather than replace it with a new one. Not only does this make good practical and economic sense, but you're also preserving as much of the original building as possible.

Top Tip

■ ■ ■ ■ ■ ■ ■ ■ ■ ■ ■ ■

For information on the sensitive restoration of listed buildings contact the Society for the Protection of Ancient Buildings or the Listed Properties Owners Club (see pages 188 and 190).

■ ■ ■ ■ ■ ■ ■ ■ ■ ■ ■ ■

2   **Employ experts.** Some jobs in a period home, such as thatching or stonemasonry, should be left to the experts. Don't get out of your depth or you could devalue your property.

3   **Use authentic materials.** Modern building materials are often incompatible with the needs of old buildings, so use only those that are faithful to your property. For example, if you need to replace plasterwork, use a lime plaster that lets your old building breathe, absorbs condensation and allows damp to evaporate. And as lime is a relatively soft material, it can accommodate the slight movements that traditional buildings often experience.

4   **Do your homework.** Immerse yourself in books about architectural

history and traditional building construction. You might not want to do any of the hands-on restoration yourself, but you should be knowledgeable about the subject and fully involved in the decision-making process. Putting the wrong period features back in is as bad as taking the originals out.

5 Learn to love your local planner. Whether your house is listed or not, it's important to keep up a good relationship with planning and conservation officers. They can make or break your plans for restoration. They'll also have an excellent idea of which kind of period features your home would have had originally.

If you do need to employ a professional, it can be difficult to know where to start. If you have a listed building, you'll already know that any repairs have to be made like-with-like, using historically accurate materials and methods. But even if your house isn't listed, it's still important to try to restore it using traditional skills and tools.

Most builders can whip up a breeze-block wall or reskim a ceiling to perfection, but few know the intricacies of re-creating cornicing or how to rethatch a roof. And who can blame them? Demand for this kind of work has been pretty rare – until now.

Thanks to TV programmes such as *Restoration Village* and *Grand Designs*, more and more people are taking on period properties and trying to revive their features. This, coupled with the fact that local authorities are red hot about preserving the character of listed buildings, has meant that conservation builders and other traditional tradesmen are in high demand.

One of the best places to start genning up is the fantastic Building Conservation website (see page 184), where you can find conservation experts and tradesmen, read articles on everything from dry rot to rising damp, and find courses and events, as well as buy books covering the history and repair of historic buildings. Another great resource is the Period Property website (see page 189), which has a huge directory of craftsmen and professionals to help you enhance your period home, as well as advice on buying, selling, insuring, restoring and researching your house. A quick search and you'll find blacksmiths, stonemasons, cob builders, dry stone wallers, French polishers, granite and marble suppliers, lime plasterers, locksmiths, stained glass experts and master thatchers to name but a few.

Unlike normal tradesmen, who can reassure clients by joining one of the associations such as the Federation of Master Builders, conservation experts tend to work alone. Professional or trade associations do exist, such as the Dry Stone Walling Association and the Guild of Architectural Ironmongers, but the best way to reassure yourself that a conservation builder or craftsman is reliable is to see examples of his or her past work and ask for references. Luckily, the building conservation world is a small one, and most shady practitioners are soon found out and discredited. Equally, you'll also find that most historic building specialists will be more than happy to recommend other experts in different fields.

Period features checklist

Before work starts

■ Research the history of your home and try to discover which period features are missing.

■ Talk to an estate agent about potential value gain.

■ Check with your local planning officer or Building Control officer if you plan any major works, such as electrics or replacing windows.

■ Talk to the Listed Buildings officer if your home is listed and make an application for Listed Buildings Consent.

■ Research the costs of buying appropriate period features from salvage yards or getting reproductions made.

■ Do your cost/profit calculations, then secure the finances.

■ Choose a conservation expert, if you are planning to employ one.

■ Inform your home insurance company about the impending building work, especially if you are DIYing (any tradesmen or contractors should have their own public liability insurance, but double-check this).

During the build

■ Protect the fabric of the building so that nothing is damaged during the restoration process.

■ Expect regular visits from the Building Control officer if you have applied for Building Regulations approval.

■ Keep a tight check on the budget.

After the project is completed

■ Expect a final inspection from the Building Control officer, and ask for a Completion Certificate (if required) to be issued. The Listed Buildings officer might want to come and inspect the final results.

■ Pay the tradesmen in full only when you are completely satisfied with the work. Ask for any guarantees to be issued.

■ Get an estate agent to revalue your home, then inform your insurance company/mortgage provider of the new value.

chapter 7

redecoration

It never used to be the case that buyers were bothered about a new lick of paint. In fact, estate agents often recommended that home-owners absolutely did *not* decorate, as most buyers would only want to redecorate once they moved in.

Times have changed. Home-buyers these days tend to be 'cash rich, time poor' – in other words, they'd rather pay for the privilege of having a ready-decorated home than waste a weekend getting splattered with paint. In fact, research from the Alliance & Leicester building society found that nearly 80 per cent of buyers are looking for a property that requires little or no redecorating – great news for budding property developers.

The market is also more sophisticated than it used to be. Thanks to interiors and property programmes on television, most home-owners have a good sense of what buyers are looking for when it comes to decoration. It might not be to your taste, but there's no escaping the fact that colour is no longer king when it comes to selling your home. Neutrals and off-whites are the name of the game. So to summarise, here's why redecorating pays:

■ A well-presented, freshly decorated home appeals to four times as many buyers as a house that needs serious TLC.

■ Buyers will reduce their offer based on what it would cost to redecorate, but you stand to make more than your outlay if you do it yourself (see 'Costs versus profit' below).

■ Buyers usually find it easier to imagine themselves in a neutral colour scheme. You risk alienating buyers if your home is too personal.

Costs versus profit

According to recent research by the Halifax, redecorating is the most popular home improvement carried out in the hope that it adds value. In the survey over a third of people who had redecorated their home believed that their efforts had added up to £2500 to the value of their property, and almost one in three thought it would add between £2500 and £10,000.

It's difficult to quantify how much redecorating your house will add as there are so many factors involved, including quality of paint, quality of finish and size of house, but what we can say is that repainting your home is probably the cheapest way to add value to it. And, just as importantly, a freshly decorated home will certainly help your house to sell more quickly and for the asking price.

Depending on who you speak to, estimates vary as to how much value repainting a house will add. At the conservative end of the spectrum you can expect to add around £1000–£2000, while a fantastic paint job in a large property could add up to 10 per cent of the value. It might be easier to think about repainting in terms of a return on your investment. In this case, it's not unreasonable to expect between 200 and 300 per cent on your outlay.

■ The wrong colours or wallpapers can make a room feel smaller or squatter than it really is.

■ Light colours will make your home feel brighter and cleaner, which, in turn, attracts a better chance of an offer.

■ According to research conducted by the Alliance & Leicester, women are more put off than men by non-neutral decor. Appealing to women is essential if you want to sell your home, as they tend to have the final say in most house-buying partnerships.

Do I need planning permission or Building Regulations?

No. Any internal decorating, such as wallpapering, replacing skirting boards or painting, will not require planning permission or a Building Regulations application.

There is scope in the law to prevent home-owners from using certain internal finishes, but this would apply only if they posed a serious risk to health or safety. Lead paint comes into

Example

Say your home is worth £200,000 and you spend £2000 on basic redecoration, including walls, ceilings and woodwork. With any luck, you can expect to add between £4000 and £6000 to the asking price, making a tidy profit of £2000–£4000 in return for your efforts.

However, as always there is a proviso to this: you must get an excellent finish. Most people think that painting and decorating are a doddle. The reality is that they involve as much skill as any other DIY job. You need to be meticulous in your attention to detail, eliminating drips and streaks, and it's also vital to protect floors and other surfaces from spatters. A bad paint job will look disastrous, and will certainly knock value off your home. If you are in any doubt about whether you have the skill to do an adequate paint job, call in the professionals. You won't make any money on your outlay, but you'll certainly break even, and your house will be eminently more saleable as a result.

this category, and its use is banned in most domestic environments because it is a known health hazard. There is, however, an exception to this rule: UK regulations allow the use of lead paint in controlled and special circumstances for the redecoration of Grade I and II* listed historic buildings. Strict regulations apply to its use, so it's always important to follow the manufacturer's instructions.

Listed Buildings Consent

You might need Listed Buildings Consent if you own a listed building and want to paint brickwork, stonework, beams, fireplaces and suchlike. There may also be restrictions on the colours or types of paint you can use. This applies especially to any external decoration, but it's worth checking with the conservation officer at your local council before you start work inside or outside.

Making the best of redecoration

Don't let a poor paint job spoil your chance of a house sale. Some simple tips will help you to create a clean, crisp finish without having to call in the professionals.

Don't leave it till the last minute

It can be tempting to leave redecorating until just before you put the house on the market to ensure it's in tip-top condition. However, buyers will smell a rat if there's the whiff of fresh paint in the air, and might be put off if they think you have spruced up the house with the sole purpose of getting a higher price. Gloss paint can emit fumes for days after application, so leave at least two weeks between finishing the paintwork and inviting buyers into your home. Surveyors will also be suspicious if they sense you are trying to cover up imperfections with a new lick of paint. The key is to make your home feel as if it looks airy, bright and well maintained.

Top Tip

■ ■ ■ ■ ■ ■ ■ ■ ■ ■ ■ ■ ■

The Paint Quality Institute (see page 189) has an excellent 'paint job cost calculator', which can work out how much you're likely to spend based on factors such as price per litre and room size.

■ ■ ■ ■ ■ ■ ■ ■ ■ ■ ■ ■ ■

Glossary

VOCs

Volatile Organic Compounds (VOCs) are chemicals that evaporate from paints, varnishes, thinners and brush cleaners. Some VOCs are highly toxic and have been linked to allergies, respiratory disease, headaches and other health problems. Environmental regulations recently forced manufacturers to make significant reductions in their paints' VOC content. Always use the lowest VOC paint you can, or choose a non-toxic alternative.

Lots of companies have started selling paints that are low in or free of VOCs. Auro UK, Georgina Barrow, Earthborn, Ecos and Nutshell (see pages 183–9) are some of the more well known, and their products can be easily obtained via mail order or the internet. Farrow & Ball also produce a range called Estate Emulsion, which has good eco-credentials.

Cost the job

There's a huge range of paints on the market, varying hugely in quality and price. Below you'll see why it's important to choose good-quality paint, but it's also important not to overspend on your budget.

Think about colours and finishes

If you are putting your property on the market, the paint job you give it has two main purposes – to neutralise and depersonalise. Basically, that means turning your home into a blank canvas upon which potential buyers can imagine their furniture and possessions. For this purpose, plain colours work best, and they rule out the possibility that you'll choose a pattern that clashes with prospective buyers' furnishings. Pale, neutral colours work best – creams, off-whites and natural shades, such as stone. Brilliant white is best avoided, however, as it tends to reflect and reveal every imperfection in plaster or woodwork. It's also too institutional.

As well as providing a backdrop for buyers' furniture, pale colours also create a visual illusion. Dark colours absorb natural light, making a room feel small and intimate, whereas pale colours reflect light back into a room,

Top Tip

■ ■

Here's a trick that will leave your home looking professionally decorated. Interior designers often use different shades of the same colour to create interest. Choose one colour – cream, perhaps. Paint the ceiling in the lightest shade, the walls in the next shade darker, the dado darker still, and the woodwork in the darkest shade.

■ ■

making it feel brighter and larger. It can be fantastic using dark colours in your own home, but if you're keen to sell, your number one priority has to be to create a feeling of space.

Another decorators' tip for creating the illusion of space is to use the same colour throughout a house. It might sound monotonous, but continuous colour creates a sense of flow and movement through a home. It works especially well in small houses.

While colour and shade of paint are important, so is the finish. Flat colours tend to work better than high-gloss finishes, as they provide a softer, more forgiving effect. As a general rule, you'll need matt emulsion for the walls and ceilings, and either eggshell or satinwood paint for woodwork and metal. In rooms that get a lot of wear and tear or condensation choose

a wipeable emulsion with a bit more durability. In general, the shinier the paint, the more hardwearing it tends to be.

Choose good-quality paint

Trade paint is cheap, but what you save in money you can spend in time trying to get a good finish. Poor-quality paint tends to need a greater number of coats and never has the depth of colour achieved with better-quality paint. It's also easier to mark and will need frequent touch-ups.

Good-quality paints have highly pigmented formulations that look fantastic but can be pricey. For most houses, a mid-priced paint from a reputable manufacturer will probably do the job nicely. However, if you live in a listed building, period home or high-end property, you might want to invest in more expensive paint as this is the finish buyers will be expecting.

Prepare properly

Preparation is everything when it comes to painting. Take down any curtains, move the furniture or cover it in dust sheets, and protect the floor with plastic sheeting. Use masking tape to cover the edges of any switches or sockets, or unscrew them (making sure that the electricity is turned off at the main). Mask around or remove any doorknobs or handles too.

If you are painting the walls or ceilings, fill any cracks first and remove any dust. Woodwork will need to be sugar-soaped or lightly sanded to provide a key for the undercoat. (If you are painting a room with all new materials, such as fresh plaster or bare wood, you'll need to start with a coat of appropriate primer on everything.)

Do things in the right order

Decorators tend to paint a room from top to bottom: that means ceiling first, followed by walls, then woodwork. The logic of this is that you won't drip paint on to any wet painted surfaces. Wait for each stage to dry properly before starting the next.

Use good tools

If you buy good-quality brushes and rollers, the job should take less time and you'll have fewer unsightly brush marks. Quality brushes give you a thicker, more uniform finish that not only looks better, but is more resistant to dirt and mould. According to the Paint Quality Institute, you'll need:

- 30–50 mm brushes for trims;
- 50–80 mm brushes for doors;
- 100 mm brushes for floors and small expanses of wall;
- 150 mm brushes for large expanses of wall;
- angled brush for detailed painting, such as sash window frames.

Buying a good-quality roller is also vital. Quality rollers have a thicker pile, which allows them to hold more paint and makes them less prone to drips. They also apply the paint more thickly and smoothly. Choose a short-pile roller (6–9 mm) for walls and ceilings, and a long-pile roller (12–25 mm) for bricks and rough masonry.

Check the room temperature

Paint is radically affected by external conditions, and you'll get a much better finish if your room is at the correct temperature. Too cold (5°C/40°F or less) and the paint will take too long to dry, making it more likely to run or pick up dust; too hot (over 30°C/86°F or in direct sunshine) and the paint can dry too quickly, causing it to crack or flake and become less durable.

Forget paint effects

Stippling, feathering, sponging, combing, rag-rolling, stencilling – the 1980s were awash with paint effects. Unfortunately, these now look a bit dated. If you've got them, get rid of them. If you haven't, don't be tempted.

Final touch-up

You've finished the job, so stand back and admire your handiwork. Now's the time to be super-critical: do you need to do a few touch-ups here and there? Have you removed all the paint from the window panes? Are there any splashes or drips where they don't belong? Be ruthless because the buyer certainly will.

Redecoration checklist

■ Talk to your estate agent about potential value gains.

■ Cost the job using a paint calculator.

■ Use the best paint and tools you can afford.

■ Stick to neutral colour schemes.

■ Protect your furnishings, mask off windows and switches, and prepare the surfaces.

■ Apply a primer coat if needed.

■ Work top down, using emulsion, then gloss.

■ Paint at the correct temperature.

■ Get a neat finish and do a final touch-up.

chapter 8

conservatories

Conservatories are very popular in the UK. They're a great way of bridging the gap between house and garden, allowing you to enjoy the views without worrying about the weather. They're also a fairly straightforward way of adding space and potential value to your home.

Why a conservatory?

■ Conservatories can make a home feel lighter and brighter, without compromising on warmth and comfort.

■ They give you greater enjoyment of the outside, blurring the boundary between garden and living space.

■ Conservatories are a blank canvas, making them a great multi-use space.

■ They are a relatively inexpensive way of adding floor space.

■ They don't tend to need planning permission.

■ Construction is quick and usually causes minimal disruption

Is it right for my house?

Not all homes suit a conservatory, especially if the garden is small or the outlook is a bit gloomy. Here are a few pointers to help you decide whether to go ahead.

Top Tip

■ ■ ■ ■ ■ ■ ■ ■ ■ ■ ■ ■ ■

When you are budgeting for your conservatory, remember to factor in the cost of putting the garden right. Trees, plants and hard landscaping, such as access paths and patios, will be essential to the enjoyability and utility of the space.

■ ■ ■ ■ ■ ■ ■ ■ ■ ■ ■ ■ ■

■ Location is everything. An attractive, well-constructed conservatory will certainly add value in a popular area. Research by the bank Egg found that some parts of the country saw higher value gains on conservatories than others – East Anglia, the east Midlands, Scotland and London all ranked

Costs versus profit

The general consensus is that, done properly, a conservatory will add about 5 per cent to the value of your house.

Example

If your house is worth £200,000, the maximum value you could add with a conservatory is around £10,000. Conservatories can cost as little as £3000 or as much as £50,000. How much you spend should depend on where you live and the inherent value of your home.

well above the average 5 per cent. East Anglian residents, for example, reaped an average £19,000. The southeast, northwest and Yorkshire/Humberside all saw an average £10,000 value gain, while Wales and the north struggled to add more than £5000–£8000. What can we deduce from these figures? First, in none of the regions did the addition of a conservatory cause an average house to lose value. However, there were definitely areas of the UK that proved more profitable. The reason for London's success is probably down to the sheer demand for floor space and extra rooms in the country's capital. It's also vital to make the most of outside space in such an urban environment. But conservatories also seem to add value in rural areas, where houses back on to open spaces, hence the success of East Anglia, the east Midlands and Scotland.

The key is to use your common sense. If building a conservatory will allow you greater enjoyment and use of your outside space, it's worth building. If you don't want to draw attention to your outside space – perhaps the views are ugly, the garden is tiny, or your neighbour's garden is unsightly – it's probably best to leave well alone. Always talk to an estate agent first to see whether they agree with your proposals. They'll know the ins and outs of the area, and whether a conservatory is an investment worth making.

Consider the following key questions before making a decision.

How old is your home?

The age of a building doesn't necessarily dictate *whether* you should have a conservatory, but it should influence the type of conservatory you build. A conservatory must be in keeping with the style and age of your house. Those made of uPVC look terrible on period properties, and if your home is listed, there's a strong chance you won't be able to erect one anyway.

How near are your neighbours?

The planning rules detail how close you can build a conservatory to an adjoining house, but you have to think about how your plans will affect the people on either side of your property. A conservatory near a boundary can cause particular problems for privacy. A solid wall or obscure glazing on the boundary side can help, but then you have issues such as right-to-light and overshadowing. There are also practical issues, such as how you are going to clean the glass or make repairs if you build next to a boundary wall.

How big is your home?

If you already have plenty of downstairs living space, it's unlikely that you'll add much value with the addition of a conservatory. If you do go ahead, buyers will expect a very high standard of conservatory if you have a substantial home; this might compromise any potential profit you were hoping for. Equally, if your home is tiny, there's a good chance that you would make a better investment if you extended rather than added on a conservatory: a downstairs that consists of just a small living room, galley kitchen and large conservatory would feel out of balance.

How big is your garden?

While adding floor space tends to add value, it doesn't if it compromises the garden space. You have to weigh up the balance between conservatory size and remaining garden. Remember, a family-sized house needs a family-sized garden. A reduction in the garden area could actually devalue your property in spite of the extra floor space you've created.

How big do you want to build?

Most people overestimate the size of conservatory they need, which can lead to a poorly proportioned, difficult-

The style of conservatory you choose should reflect the style of your home. Here a modern conservatory complements a modern property.

to-heat room. Richmond Oak Bespoke Conservatories offers great advice for working out how big to build. First, measure some of the rooms in your home and look at how much furniture you have in the space. (The average room size in the UK is around 16 square metres, and slightly less than this in a newly built property.) The next step is to get outside with some bricks, string or lengths of wood and dummy up the size of the conservatory you would like on the ground, marking the positions of doors from the house and into the garden. Finally, they suggest you arrange some garden furniture in your outlined space so that you can see how the thoroughfares work, and assess how comfortably you can move around your furniture and how much space you need.

Where will I park my car?

A conservatory should not compromise your provision for car parking, or cause road safety problems for you or your neighbours. Will you be able to manoeuvre your car safely if you go ahead with the extension?

Where will the conservatory go?

A conservatory should be confined to the rear or side elevations. Front con-

The treated but unpainted timber of this rustic conservatory is perfectly in keeping with a period property.

servatories will almost never get planning permission, unless you look out on to your own land. What direction will your conservatory face? A south-facing conservatory will get lots of light, but will almost certainly need plenty of ventilation and shade during the summer. A north-facing one will be cooler in summer, but even colder in winter, so think about methods of heating the room.

Is it right for my family?

■ Conservatories have many of the benefits of an extension, so they are ideal for growing families who need extra space but don't want to face the upheaval of moving. They can make useful office spaces, dining rooms, family rooms or playrooms.

■ Conservatories can be a blessing for people who suffer from mobility problems. The light and airy space is ideal for infirm family members, who might not otherwise be able to get outside to enjoy the benefits of a garden.

■ Conservatories are ideal places for tasks that require natural light. They can be wonderful workrooms and studios for artists, as well as excellent spaces for conducting hobbies and craft activities.

■ With careful planning, conservatories also make excellent kitchens. What could be better than preparing a meal or sipping a glass of wine while enjoying glorious views of the garden?

Will I need planning permission?

Whether or not you need planning permission depends entirely on your plans. You will need to apply for permission if:

■ your house is listed;
■ you live in a flat or maisonette;
■ your conservatory will be nearer the highway than your original house, unless there's 20 metres between your house (as extended) and the highway (note that the term 'highway' includes all public roads, footpaths, bridleways and byways);
■ your conservatory (and any other outbuildings) will cover more than half of your garden.

You will also need to apply for permission if your conservatory exceeds the following limits:

Height limits for conservatories

■ If the conservatory extension is higher than the highest part of the

Top Tip

■ ■

Keep an eye out for changes in planning laws. A shake-up of the current system was recently proposed by the government, with the intention of speeding up the process of getting planning permission. Minor domestic projects, such as conservatories, may no longer need planning permission if there is little impact on neighbours.

■ ■

roof of the original house, you'll need planning permission.

■ If any part of the conservatory is more than 4 metres high and is within 2 metres of the boundary of your property, you'll also need permission.

Volume limits for conservatories

■ For a terraced house, or any house in a Conservation Area, a National Park or an Area of Outstanding Natural Beauty, if the volume of the original house would be increased by more than 10 per cent or 50 cubic metres (whichever is the greater), you'll need planning permission.

■ For any other kind of house outside those areas, if the volume of the original house would be increased by more than 15 per cent or 70 cubic metres (whichever is the greater), you'll need planning permission.

Note: When calculating the volume of your house or a conservatory, it's the external rather than the internal volume that is required. If you already have other buildings in your garden, these might be counted against your volume allowance. Always talk to your local planning department first.

What about Building Regulations?

You *do not* need Building Regulations if your conservatory meets all the following conditions:

■ It must be single storey and at ground level.

■ It must be less than 30 square metres internally.

■ It must be separated from your original house by windows and doors that can be closed off from the original house when not in use (see below, Example 1 – Ground Floor).

- At least half the area of the walls should be glazed.
- At least half the area of the roof should be glazed or covered in a translucent material.

- All radiators within the conservatory are controllable.
- The glazing satisfies energy-loss and safety requirements as specified by Building Regulations.
- Any electrics and plumbing comply with Building Regulations.
- It does not contain any drainage facilities, such as a sink or toilet.

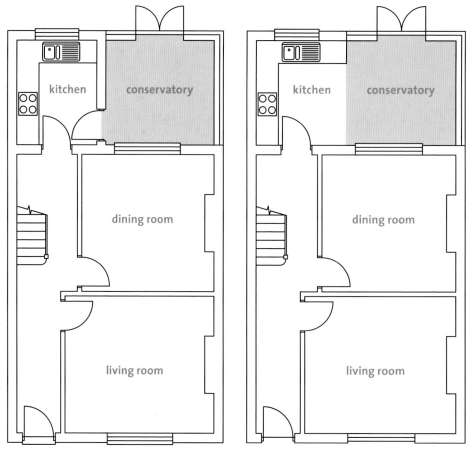

Example 1   **Example 2**

You *do* need Building Regulations approval if:

■ The conservatory is not separated from the house by windows and doors, and therefore counted as an extension (see opposite, Example 2 – Ground Floor).

■ You need to form a new or wider opening in the wall of the original house – this counts as a structural alteration and needs checking by your local Building Control officer.

■ You want to put drainage into your conservatory to create a kitchen/conservatory.

Boundary Regulations

There are a number of considerations when it comes to building a conservatory near or next to a neighbour's boundary. Planners will take into account such things as how far the conservatory will project into the garden, whether any parts of the conservatory will overhang your neighbours' land, whether the foundations will affect your neighbours' property, and whether your conservatory will affect your neighbours' amenity and enjoyment of their land. Talk through the proposals with your local planning department – there may be local

Glossary

By-laws

By-laws are rules adopted by an organisation in order to regulate its affairs and the behaviour of its members. In the case of planning, by-laws usually refer to rules set down by a local authority that are specific to the region.

covenants or by-laws that you need to take into consideration. It's also good manners to talk to your neighbours about your plans, especially if they involve a party wall or require access to your neighbour's garden for installation purposes.

Making best use of the space

Unfortunately, many conservatories fail to live up to their promise. Inadequate heating, drafty windows and baking hot summers can often make the space uninhabitable. Here are a few tips for creating a conservatory that you can enjoy all year round.

Always go for a glass roof

Don't be tempted to scrimp and fit a cheap polycarbonate roof. Plastic

roofs tend to look cheap, discolour quickly and provide very limited sound insulation in a downpour. One of their biggest drawbacks, however, is that polycarbonate roofs tend to have very poor temperature control, leaving your conservatory freezing in winter and boiling hot in summer. With the introduction of energy efficiency ratings as part of the new HIPs (see page 17), it's worth making sure your conservatory's heating loss doesn't let you down.

Think about how you'll clean it

It's a fact of life that your conservatory will collect dust and grime. It can be very time-consuming to clean the glass by hand, and almost impossible to get regular access to the roof, so think about self-cleaning glass. Brands such as Pilkington Activ™ have a dual-action coating that helps the glass to shed any dirt.

Spend money where it counts

While you can pick up uPVC kits for a few thousand pounds, there's no doubt that hardwood conservatories look more attractive. If you live in a Conservation Area, or your home is listed, you might be allowed to install only a wood conservatory. It's also important to install good-quality foundations, insulation and double glazing. Skimp on those and you'll only end up spending more on heating and cooling systems throughout the year.

Hardwearing floor

It can be tricky choosing flooring for a conservatory. On the one hand you want it to be a cosy and comfortable living space; on the other hand you need the floor to be hardwearing and able to withstand muddy shoes from the garden. Tiles and flagstones are an elegant solution, but can be cold, so opt for under-floor heating or washable rugs to soften the room. Lino and wood flooring are also good options, especially if they provide continuity with the rest of the house. Carpets are another option, but you'll have to search around for a brand that is suitable for areas of high traffic, stain resistant and, most important, resistant to sunlight. The strength of daylight in most conservatories is enough to fade virtually any colour.

Heating and blinds

Some conservatories don't feel like part of the house, often because the temperature is radically different from that in other rooms, or because the space lacks any real privacy. It's vital that you attempt to control the temperature in the conservatory: in winter you'll need adequate heating in the form of radiators or under-floor heating; in summer you'll need to think about ventilation and the benefits of heat-reflecting glass. Blinds are also a must for any conservatory. Not only will they help prevent heat loss and provide shade, but they'll also allow you privacy during the evenings.

Think about the flow from the rest of the house

There are several ways to stop the conservatory feeling like an add-on. Run the same flooring from the adjacent room and make the conservatory floor height the same as the floors in your home. Keep the colours similar and continue any themes from other rooms into the conservatory. Choose furniture that doesn't obscure the views into the garden – glass tables and low-backed sofas are ideal.

Outside appeal

Always try to tie your new conservatory into the exterior of your home. Match stone, brick and render details, and pick out interesting architectural features, such as window design and bargeboards.

DIY or get the professionals in?

Competent DIYers could attempt many elements of building a conservatory without too much bother, and save themselves hundreds, if not thousands, in the process. Most of the initial work is simply hard graft – excavating the trenches for the foundations, for example, or mixing and laying the concrete base. Other jobs are equally straightforward, including laying the hardcore and blinding layer of sand, cutting out a damp-proof membrane, and adding any floor insulation. Other tasks that affect the finish of the job, such as laying bricks and erecting the frame or glazing panels, should be attempted only if you are confident that you can get a neat finish. A badly built, leaky conservatory will be a disaster for both your home and your finances.

Conservatory checklist

Before work starts

■ Check that your home is suitable for a conservatory in terms of garden space, views, proximity to neighbouring boundaries and so forth.

■ Plan what you'd like to include, such as blinds, flooring, plumbing, heating.

■ Talk to an estate agent about potential value gain.

■ Get three quotes from appropriate manufacturers, or search for a good off-the-shelf deal.

■ Do your cost/profit calculations, then secure the finances.

■ Choose your specialist contractor (who will provide plans), or consult an architect, or draw up your own building plans.

■ You probably won't need planning permission or Building Regulations, but check with your local council first. Also make sure that your plans don't cause any boundary or right-to-light issues.

■ Inform your home insurance company about the impending building work, especially if you are DIYing (any conservatory company should have its own public liability insurance, but double-check this).

During the build

■ Expect regular visits from the Building Control officer if you have applied for Building Regulations approval.

■ Keep a tight check on the budget.

After the project is completed

■ Expect a final inspection from the Building Control officer, and ask for a Completion Certificate to be issued if needed.

■ Pay the tradesmen in full only when you are completely satisfied with the work. Ask for any guarantees to be issued.

■ Get an estate agent to revalue your home.

■ If necessary, inform your home insurance company/mortgage provider that the work is complete and of the new value of your home.

chapter 9

gardens and roof terraces

In a country that has between 150 and 200 rainy days every year, it's amazing that we spend so much effort looking after our gardens. As buyers, we put an absolute premium on having somewhere to relax outdoors, even if it's just a balcony or roof terrace. In fact, in a 2006 survey commissioned by Saga it was revealed that an overwhelming 82 per cent of us said that having a garden or outside space was the most important feature when house-hunting. But what is it exactly about well-kept gardens that appeals, and why does it matter to have access to an outside space?

■ Gardens provide an important extension to the home, allowing us a living space that has the sole purpose of giving us pleasure. Gardens are where we entertain friends, relax and unwind, play with our children and seek solitude.

■ Gardening is a national passion. We buy the books, watch the TV programmes and at least three-quarters of us spend once a week tending our plots.

■ Gardens are restorative places, essential to human well-being. We might not be aware of it, but endless research has shown that contact with the natural world improves mental well-being and aids relaxation.

■ Gardens and outside spaces provide a view from the inside of our homes. An untidy garden will spoil even the smartest of interior schemes. From the outside looking in, gardens also provide a 'frame' or backdrop for our houses.

■ Gardens and outside spaces provide a physical and metaphorical 'buffer' between houses, preventing home-owners feeling overlooked or squashed together.

■ If you live in a city, a garden creates a little bit of countryside on your doorstep. Gardens also have an important cooling effect on urban areas – concrete and tarmac retain heat and can create city microclimates as much as 5°C/40°F warmer than surrounding suburbs. Plants, through transpiration, directly cool the air, and can reduce surface temperatures dramatically.

■ Your garden is the first thing house-hunters will see. You don't want to jeopardise a sale before they've even stepped through the door. According to an Alliance & Leicester survey, men are particularly put off by a poorly maintained garden.

■ Research conducted by property-finder.com revealed that more than half of the house-hunters they asked would not return for a second viewing to a house with an unkempt garden. Over 80 per cent wouldn't return if the garden had been concreted over.

Do I need planning permission or Building Regulations?

In general, the answer is 'no'. Most sheds, greenhouses, summer-houses and ponds can be constructed without the need for planning permission. However, some exceptions, as specified opposite, do apply.

Costs versus profit

The Royal Institute of Chartered Surveyors estimates that an attractive, well-maintained, good-sized garden can add between 5 and 10 per cent to the value of your house.

Example

Let's say your house is worth £200,000. Giving your garden a make-over could potentially add between £10,000 and £20,000, so it's important to make sure you don't spend more than this if you want to add value.

What you do to your garden will influence how much value you add. Simply giving the lawn a quick mow won't add megabucks, but neither will erecting a huge folly. The key is to create an attractive, simple garden that's easy to maintain and looks good for as much of the year as possible. It's vital that you don't intimidate house-hunters with a garden that looks like a lot of effort to maintain – most people don't have the time or the resources to keep up a 'show garden'.

1 Structures including sheds, summer-houses and greenhouses

You will need to apply for planning permission if:

- you want to put up a structure that would be nearer to any highway than the nearest part of the original house, unless there would be at least 20 metres between the new building and any highway;
- more than half the area of land around the house would be covered by additions or other buildings;
- the structure is not to be used for domestic purposes, such as storing goods in connection with a business;
- the structure is more than 3 metres high, or more than 4 metres high if it has a ridged roof;
- you live in a listed building, a Conservation Area, a National Park, or an Area of Outstanding Natural Beauty and you want to put up a structure with a volume of more than 10 cubic metres.

2 Fences, walls and gates

You will need to apply for planning permission if:

■ the fence, wall or gate would be over 1 metre high and next to a highway used by vehicles (or the footpath of such a highway), or over 2 metres high elsewhere;

■ your house is a listed building or in the curtilage of a listed building.

In a Conservation Area you might also need consent to take down a fence, wall or gate. Elsewhere, you will not need permission to take down a fence, wall or gate, or to alter or improve an existing fence, wall or gate, as long as you don't increase the height.

3 Trees

Well-established trees are often protected by Tree Preservation Orders, so you'll need your local council's consent to prune or fell them. There are also controls over many other trees in Conservation Areas. Always check with your council before you take on any arboricultural work.

4 Hedges

You do not need planning permission for hedges. However, if a planning condition or a covenant restricts planting, you might need planning permission and/or other consent.

Since November 2003 there has been legislation to deal with the prob-

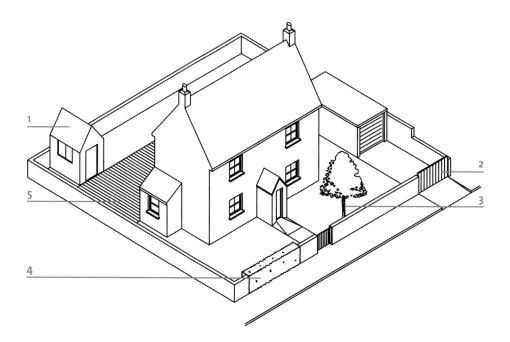

lem of excessively high evergreen hedges. If your neighbour's hedge is adversely affecting the reasonable enjoyment of your property you can complain to the local council.

Glossary

Tree Preservation Order

Planning authorities have powers to protect trees by making a Tree Preservation Order (TPO). This makes it an offence to cut down, top, lop, uproot, wilfully damage or destroy any protected tree(s) without first having obtained permission from the local authority. All types of tree can be protected, whether as single trees or as part of a woodland, copse or other grouping of trees. Protection does not, however, extend to hedges, bushes or shrubs.

5 Patios and decking

There are no planning restrictions for any size area of patio provided that it is for domestic purposes. Driveways do not count as patios, so they are subject to permission (see Garages and Parking, page 153).

Decking is usually exempt from planning, but there are exceptions, including where the deck is situated within 20 metres of a highway; where the deck is at first-floor level or above; if any part of the deck construction exceeds 3 metres in height; and if the deck is attached to a listed building or situated in a Conservation Area or National Park.

As always, be sure to talk to your local planning department before you start work.

Making the best of the garden

Gardening can be an expensive hobby, so it's vital you get the most from your budget. Choosing the right plants, creating areas of interest, and keeping on top of the maintenance will ensure that your investment reaps the maximum reward.

Love your lawn

Most buyers will expect a lawned area, however small. Not only does it break up the garden, helping to highlight the plants and trees, but it also offers a valuable recreational space for children and adults alike. If you need to start a lawn from scratch, you have two choices – seed or turf. Seed

Top Tip

■ ■

If you're sprucing up your garden with a view to putting your house on the market, consider what it will look like at different times of the year. Make sure that there will be colour and interest during all the seasons, not just spring and summer.

■ ■

is the cheaper option, but takes longer to produce results. Turf is more expensive, but provides instant results, which may be essential if you're about to put the house on the market. If you already have a lawn but it's looking a bit tired, here's how to get it back in tip-top condition:

■ Reseed or returf any bare patches.

■ Keep the grass watered during long dry spells. A week of strong sun is enough to yellow your lawn, so get the sprinkler out. Water only in the early morning or late evening, or the sun and water droplets will combine to scorch the grass.

■ Feed it. A lawn has different feeding requirements depending on the time of year. Your garden centre should have seasonal fertilisers especially for this purpose.

■ Mow once a week between March and October. Don't be tempted to cut the grass too short or it will turn brown. A height of 2.5 cm is ideal. Grass should also be dry when you mow, and always remove the cuttings, as they tend to impede aeration and encourage disease. Grass growth slows during the winter, so mow only occasionally and when the weather is mild.

■ Trim the edges. Keep the borders looking neat by trimming the edge of the lawn about every two weeks during the growing season.

Choose low-maintenance plants

Home-buyers will panic if they see a garden that requires lots of upkeep. Choose plants that can take care of themselves, and be sure to point this out to any prospective buyers – they'll want to know how easy it is to keep the garden looking great. Five of the best are:

Lavender – a gorgeous, perfumed shrub that looks fantastic in summer, but also provides shape and interest during the rest of the year.

Mahonia – one of the few plants to have fragrant flowers in winter; a great structural plant the rest of the year, and also very hardy.

Spotted laurel – an attractive and versatile evergreen shrub, with lovely dappled leaves; thrives in most soils and tolerates both sun and shade.

Senecio – also called brachyglottis, this grey-leaved shrub provides wonderful flowers over the summer, and keeps its leaves during the winter.

Rosemary – fragrant and green all year round, with the extra bonus of pretty flowers in spring; likes full sun, but is forgiving of most conditions.

Bulbs, baskets and tubs

While evergreen trees and shrubs can provide year-round structure and background colour, it's easy to brighten up your garden with some bulbs or bedding plants. Invest in some large terracotta pots, hanging baskets or other planters and start stuffing them with seasonal colour. These will provide instant effect and can be updated every month or two, depending on what's in flower.

If you want to make a strong impression at the front of your home, standard bay trees or clipped box topiary in matching pots always look smart on either side of your door.

Create a seating area

Most home-buyers want a garden they can imagine themselves sitting in, so it's important to define an area, however small, that can accommodate a table and chairs. If the garden is tiny, a compact table with two chairs will look better than a huge family dining set. Ideally, the table and chairs should be on an area of hard standing, such as a patio or decking, but a quiet corner of your lawn can work well too. Strategically placed benches and arbours also create a welcoming effect.

Think about storage

If you have a medium-sized or larger garden, it might be worth installing a garden shed. Buyers like to see that there is a safe, secure and dry area to store garden furniture and equipment. Tidying away clutter also helps give the impression of a larger space. Sheds start from as little as a few hundred pounds and look fantastic when painted or stained. Traditional paint manufacturers Farrow & Ball have some beautiful colours in their Exterior Eggshell range, many of which were inspired by sheds, follies and other garden structures found in

The most unpromising spaces can be transformed into oases of peace and calm. And if the plants and materials are chosen carefully, maintenance can be kept to a minimum.

historic homes up and down the UK. Smaller gardens can still make the most of storage in the form of bin tidies and screens, mini-sheds, storage benches, and wooden fruit trays stacked on top of each other.

Top Tip

■ ■ ■ ■ ■ ■ ■ ■ ■ ■ ■ ■

If you don't have the budget to replace a tired-looking patio or path, a quick pressure-wash often gives surprisingly good results. Failing that, a thin layer of gravel chippings can hide a multitude of sins.

■ ■ ■ ■ ■ ■ ■ ■ ■ ■ ■ ■

Roof terraces

In the past decade roof terraces have become increasingly common in city housing, but what is it that has made them so popular?

■ Roof terraces are a great way of grabbing space from a previously redundant area for relatively little expense.

■ Many town houses and apartment blocks in urban areas have no access to private or communal gardens, so a roof terrace is often the only solution to creating a green space.

■ Apartments are often the first rung on the property ladder for young professionals, and roof terraces are ideal for them as they offer somewhere to sit in the sun without the maintenance of a garden.

Costs versus profit

A survey by the Bradford & Bingley building society showed that a flat with a roof terrace can be worth 10 per cent more than an equivalent flat without a roof terrace. If you're prepared to do most of the work yourself, you can create a roof terrace for as little as £5000. However, due to the health and safety issues of working on roofs, not to mention planning, it's much wiser to get in the professionals.

Expect to pay around £15,000 for architect's and builder's fees (or £30,000 if you live in London, which tends to be almost twice as expensive when it comes to house renovations). However, on the right home you can hope to add 10 per cent to its value. It makes good financial sense, then, if the flat is worth more than £150,000 (or £300,000 if you live in the capital).

The proviso is that your flat has to be suitable for a roof terrace. If there is already access to an outside space, a roof terrace will not add any benefit in terms of value. The best places for roof terraces are attractive but heavily populated urban centres inhabited mainly by young professionals (families with children might not want a roof terrace for safety reasons). Victorian and Georgian town houses that have been turned into flats are obvious candidates, but many other buildings, including modern apartment blocks, can be successfully transformed.

■ Roof terraces tend to be eco-friendly and money-saving. Buildings with roof gardens lose 30 per cent less heat in the winter, are cooler in the summer, and offer year-round sound insulation.

What about planning permission and Building Regulations?

There's a strong chance you'll need planning permission for a roof terrace, as the alteration affects the outside of your house and your neighbours' enjoyment of the area. However, the good news is that in urban areas planning authorities tend to take a positive view of roof gardens, as they contribute to the environment, encourage wildlife in the city, improve air quality, introduce better insulation on the building and enhance the overall appearance. Make sure your planning application makes it clear that you plan to include lots of plants and greenery as this will appeal to the planners' current thinking.

You'll certainly need Building Regulations. Roofs are not designed to take substantial weights, so you'll need to strengthen and reinforce the roof structure. You'll also need to comply with regulations about stairs and ac-

cess, fire safety and adequate rainwater drainage, among other things.

As with all major home improvements, talk to an estate agent first to get an idea of potential profit, then talk to the planning authorities to make sure your ideas are suitable. If you live in a listed building or an Area of Outstanding Natural Beauty, you'll also have to obtain extra permission. Give your local council a call before making any arrangements.

chapter 10

garages and parking

When asked, home-buyers often put private parking at the top of their wishlist – and with good reason. Many houses built before the age of motorised transport don't have adequate provision for car parking. Even in streets that do have plentiful on-street parking, it's often difficult to get a space near your own front door. According to a recent RAC survey, 17 per cent of people in England find it difficult to park outside their home. It's no wonder that private parking – either off-street or in a garage – is so popular, especially in busy, built-up areas. But what is it specifically about parking that adds or detracts from the value of your home?

Why bother?

- Due to the increased risk of theft and damage, insurance companies place a heavy penalty on motorists who keep their cars on a public road. Off-street parking or a private garage will significantly lower your insurance premium.
- According to the RAC, car parking is one of the biggest causes of rows between neighbours – at least 11 per cent of motorists reported arguments with neighbours about parking.
- As zoned parking increases, off-road parking becomes more valuable. In Westminster, for example, the council issues around 40,000 residents' parking permits annually, but has about 30,000 car parking bays. No wonder there's a battle for spaces.
- For people with mobility problems, young families and the elderly, a private parking space next to the house is absolutely vital.
- Having no off-street parking actually detracts from the saleability and value of your home.
- Apart from security, garages offer useful storage and workshop space.
- The creation of a garage and an off-street parking space tends not to require complex planning permission.
- With car ownership expected to increase up to 45 per cent by 2030, a property with its own parking will be even more desirable in the future.

Is it right for my house?

Not all houses will benefit from off-street parking. It can be tricky striking a balance between the need for a garden and the need to park your car; many homes in London, for example, have sacrificed their front gardens to create off-street parking. In other areas, such as rural Scotland, with low population numbers and plenty of space, off-street parking adds very little to the equation. So is it right for your home and street?

Is your street full of cars?

Do you always have to fight for a parking space? If so, finding the space for off-street parking might be a wise investment.

Do you have zoned parking?

That suggests a high demand for parking spaces and a premium for off-street parking and garages.

Do you have a large garden?

If so, there may be a good case for creating a parking area without spoiling the enjoyment of your outside space.

Costs versus profit

Despite the fact that the premium for private parking has fallen in the past few years, having somewhere to put your car is still a great way to add value to your home. Current figures suggest that off-street parking adds around 6 per cent to the value of your house, a single garage adds 9 per cent, and a double garage nearly 15 per cent. Conversely, lack of off-street parking knocks around 6 per cent off your property's asking price.

Example

For the average £200,000 house, you can add up to £12,000 if it has off-street parking, £18,000 with a single garage, and almost £30,000 with a smart double garage.

Cost-wise, you can create basic off-street parking for as little as £2000. Garages vary in cost from £1500 concrete prefabs to £20,000 and beyond for oak-framed buildings, so it's important not to spend more than you'll recoup. You'll also need to factor in the cost of laying concrete foundations for a garage.

Is there an existing outbuilding?

Would it be feasible to replace a redundant outbuilding (such as a shed or greenhouse) with a parking spot so that you don't lose any garden?

Does your area have a high level of car theft?

Creating secure parking could slash your insurance premiums and make your home more attractive to buyers. In central London private parking and garages can add as much as £50,000–£70,000 to the value of a home. Other cities also command high premiums. A garage in the leafy Newcastle suburb of Jesmond, for example, recently went on sale for £30,000, while a parking space in the Cornish resort of St Ives went on the market for £24,000.

What's your local council's policy?

Paving over front gardens has caused a number of flooding and drainage problems, especially in built-up areas. Your council might object if it feels that your parking plans will prevent rainwater from soaking away.

What precedent has been set in your street?

If you live in a street where no one has off-street parking or a garage, it might be difficult to break the mould.

Is your home listed?

Creating a parking area in the front garden of a listed building or a house within a Conservation Area can detract from the beauty of the property and the surrounding area. In this case, planning permission will be granted only in exceptional circumstances.

How big is your garden?

If it's small and the proposed parking takes up more than 50 per cent of the existing plot, you might struggle to get planning permission.

Do you live close to a major traffic junction?

Planners might worry about the safety of a driveway or garage near such a busy spot.

Do you have mature trees where you plan to park?

Planners will not look favourably on the creation of a drive or garage that would involve the removal of, or damage to, any mature tree in either the garden or on the pavement.

Do you live in a flat?

Permission to create parking outside shared properties is tricky as front gardens are a vital residential amenity.

Is there a covenant on your home?

Developers sometimes put clauses into the deeds that prevent you from doing anything that affects the outside appearance of your home. This is to stop home-owners making changes that lower the tone or value of an estate. Ask your solicitor to check.

Is it right for my family?

■ Think about the needs of your immediate family. If you have to make a choice, is parking or garden space more important?

■ Do you need parking spaces for frequent visitors or business clients if you work from home? If you want space for commercial vehicles, however, this will involve more complex planning issues.

■ Do you need to park near your front door because a family member has mobility issues?

- Does your routine involve a lot of loading and unloading of the car?
- Are your children reaching the age when they will want their own car? Will you need extra parking spaces?
- Do you own a car that needs to be kept dry? Classic cars are prone to rust if kept outdoors, so it's important to protect your investment and keep any valuable vehicle in dry storage. Modern cars, however, can withstand being parked in all weathers, and the money for a garage might be better spent elsewhere.
- If you need more space, would it be better to consider a two-storey extension, with parking underneath and a bedroom on top?

What about planning permission and Building Regulations?

Below you'll find a quick summary of the rules. If your house is listed or you live in a Conservation Area, the regulations will be tighter, so always speak to your local council before you embark on any changes.

1 Garages over 5 metres from the property

You do not need planning permission if the garage is to be built 5 metres or more away from the house. The garage must not be nearer to the road than the original house, and must not be more than 4 metres high (pitched

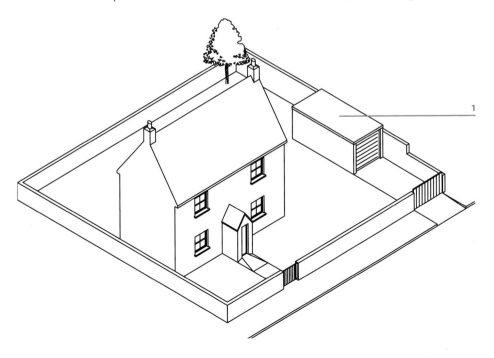

1

roof) or 3 metres high if it has a flat roof. The combined ground area of the garage and other outbuildings within the property boundary must not cover more than 50 per cent of the total garden area.

A garage is also exempt from Building Regulations provided:

■ it is detached;

■ the floor area is less than 30 square metres;

■ it is more than 1 metre from a boundary, or it is a single storey and constructed of wholly non-combustible material;

■ it contains no sleeping accommodation.

Building Regulations do not apply to a carport provided it is open on at least two sides *and* the floor area does not exceed 30 square metres.

2 Garages within 5 metres of the property

A garage less than 5 metres from the house counts as an extension and might need planning permission. If the garage adjoins the house, you will also need Building Regulation approval.

See Chapter 2 for more information on planning permission and permitted development.

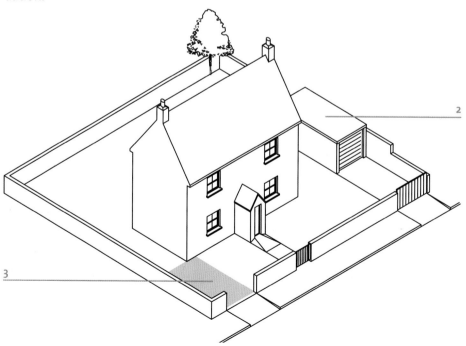

Glossary

Dropped kerb

It is illegal to build a crossing over a public footpath without a certified crossing or dropped kerb. This is to ensure that the crossing is strong enough to take the weight of the vehicle and that it does not create a hazard for pedestrians and other road users. Your council has the power to remove a vehicle crossing or dropped kerb if it has been constructed without permission. If you want to create off-road parking and this involves dropping the kerb, you can make an application to your local council's Highways Department, which will carry out the work and charge you for the costs.

3 Off-street parking

Creating off-street parking does not need planning consent as long as it doesn't involve creating access to a classified (A or B) road, is within the property's boundary, and won't be used by commercial vehicles. Note, however, that a dropped kerb might be subject to planning consent.

Making best use of the space

The following paragraphs discuss a few key points about constructing and siting a garage.

Safety

Planning regulations state what is or isn't permitted when it comes to parking, but you can save yourself a lot of time by thinking about the safety of your proposals. Will your parking space or garage cause road safety problems for you or your neighbours? Will you able to manoeuvre your car practically and safely? Will you need to reverse your car into oncoming traffic? Will your parking gates open inwards or outwards? Will any sight lines be obstructed?

Foundations and drainage

Your drive will need to take the weight of one or more cars, so must be well built. It needs to have a thick layer of hardcore, followed by a 'blinding layer' of sand or ballast to fill in the gaps in the hardcore. On top of the blinding layer you'll need either a concrete sub-layer plus your surface layer (which might be paving blocks or bricks, for example), or you can simply lay a thick layer of concrete on top of the blinding layer to provide a sturdy surface.

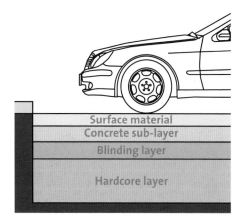

Surface material
Concrete sub-layer
Blinding layer

Hardcore layer

The thickness of the various layers will depend on the weight of the vehicles you hope to support, as well as the nature of the ground underneath your parking area. Talk to a builder about your options.

Ideally, your drive should slope away from your house to prevent water collecting against the walls or sitting on the surface of the drive. If this isn't possible, you can slope the drive towards the house and build a gully between the edge of the drive and the wall to take the water into a soakaway or surface drain. Whatever your choice, it's vital that you don't build your new driveway above the existing damp-proof course (DPC) in your house. Aim to have your drive at least 15 cm below the line of the DPC.

Size

Cars have got bigger over the years, so it's important to factor this into your calculations for a driveway or garage. A drive should be at least 3 metres wide to accommodate the opening of car doors.

A standard garage is 3 metres wide by 5 metres long, but this will not be big enough for many modern cars. An Audi 8, for example, exceeds that length, as do Bentleys, Jaguars, Daimlers, the Lexus LS430 and the

Top Tip

■ ■

Even if you don't have the money or permission for an extension, future-proof the garage by designing deeper foundations than you need. This way you can simply build upwards should the finances and planning consent materialise in the future. It's also something you can point out to any prospective buyers.

■ ■

Top Tip

■ ■ ■ ■ ■ ■ ■ ■ ■ ■ ■ ■

Check out the Garage Plans website (see page 186) to find out the size of garage needed for your make of car. It has a comprehensive list of car sizes from Alfa-Romeos to Volvos.

■ ■ ■ ■ ■ ■ ■ ■ ■ ■ ■ ■

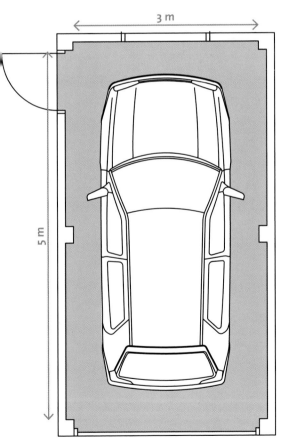

3 m

5 m

If you have a typical family car, the standard size garage leaves little room for manoeuvre or storage, so think carefully about your needs.

Mercedes S-Class. Equally, many 4 x 4s are too wide or too tall for standard-size garages. When calculating the size you require, remember to take into account the space needed for opening the doors and moving comfortably around the car. If you want extra storage space in the garage, perhaps for a freezer or workbench, you'll also need to factor this in to the equation.

Sympathy for the surroundings

Build an ugly garage and there's a good chance you'll actually knock value off your home. Pre-fab concrete garages are cheap, but they can also look unsightly, so think about ways to make the garage more in keeping with your home and street both in shape and materials. Try to match factors such as:

■ Roof type, roof pitch, tiles/slates and finish
■ Eaves and guttering
■ Wall materials and colour
■ Proportion and colour of windows and doors

Can you grow plants of different heights to soften the appearance of the garage without compromising access? Can you place the garage or parking space in a discreet area that is hidden from both the street and your outlook?

Failing that, there's always the option of taking your garage underground. An increasing number of people, especially in smart, inner city areas, are creating their own double-parking systems by stacking one space on top of another. A hydraulic system allows you to park one car at ground level, then lowers it underground; you then park your next car over the top. The costs are high – you wouldn't get much change from £40,000 – but if your house is worth towards £500,000 and you live in an area where parking is in high demand, you should see a return on your investment. A few specialist companies offer the service: see Hydraulic Parking Systems, page 187.

DIY or get the professionals in?

It's not difficult to create an area of off-street parking. Preparing the sub-base for a drive requires more brute force than brains, as most of the work is excavating soil and shovelling hardcore and concrete. The *Reader's Digest DIY Manual* has a very helpful section on calculating what depth of sub-base you'll need, depending on what kind of surface you want, as well as step-by-step instructions on how to peg out and prepare the sub-base. Laying the surface involves a little more skill, as

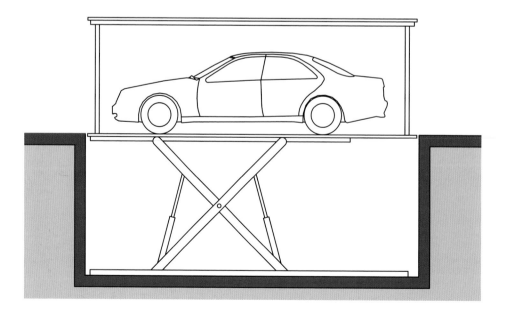

Garage and parking checklist

Before work starts

- Check that your outside space is suitable for a parking space or garage; for example, does it compromise your garden space or pedestrian safety?
- Talk to an estate agent about potential value gain.
- Get three quotes from appropriate tradesmen or contractors.
- Do your cost/profit calculations.
- Secure the finances.
- Choose your specialist contractor (who will provide plans), or consult an architect, or draw up your own building plans.
- You probably won't need planning permission and Building Regulations approval, but check with your local council first.
- Contact the Highways Department if you need to create a dropped kerb.
- Inform your home insurance company about the impending building work, especially if you are DIYing (any tradesmen or contractors should have their own public liability insurance, but double-check this).
- Arrange for alternative parking during the build.

During the build

- Keep a tight check on the budget.
- Keep an access way clear to your home.

After the project is completed

- Pay the tradesmen in full only when you are completely satisfied with the work. Ask for any guarantees to be issued.
- Get an estate agent to revalue your home.
- If necessary, inform your home insurance company/mortgage provider that the work is complete and of the new value of your home.

you'll need to ensure that it's level and attractive. Paving slabs, paving blocks, bricks and other geometric patterns should be laid carefully and bedded down properly if you want a good finish. Stone chippings and gravel are a doddle to lay, but require regular raking to look tidy. They are also not suitable for steeply sloping drives as they represent a real slipping hazard.

Competent DIYers could also tackle various aspects of the garage construction. You'll need to create a solid base, as most garages sit on concrete 10–15 cm thick. The base will also have to be about 15 cm longer and wider than the external measurements of the structure, and completely level. Always check the base specifications with the manufacturer of your garage.

Timber-framed garages are fairly straightforward to erect but you'll need at least two people for the job. The component parts of a pre-fab concrete garage are even heavier and simply too cumbersome for the average DIYer. The prices of garage kits tend to include delivery and installation anyway, so you won't be making any savings by doing it yourself. You can pick up galvanised steel self-assembly garages very cheaply – for as little as £1000 – but they tend to look a bit industrial for most housing areas.

They're also not suitable for coastal areas, where the action of salt air can have an adverse effect on the metal fabric of the building. If you have opted for a brick-built garage, you'll need to decide if your bricklaying skills are up to scratch. If you are in any doubt that the finish will be good, call in the builders.

Many houses have existing garages that need either repairing or replacing. If you already have a garage that is attached to the house and you don't use it regularly, why not consider converting it into extra living space? This doesn't usually require planning permission, but you will need to satisfy certain Building Regulations. See opposite for information about converting your garage.

Converting your garage

It's ironic that just as adding a garage can increase the value of your home, so too can converting your garage *back* into a living space. There are a few reasons for this: the first is that many garages built in the past are now not big enough to accommodate a modern family car, so end up being left empty; another is that householders tend to be so desperate for storage space that the garage is often stuffed with boxes while the car languishes on the drive. If you don't mind keeping your car outside (and most modern cars can easily withstand all weathers), then here are a few good reasons to consider swapping car space for living space.

■ Many newish houses are built on small plots, so extending into an existing garage is often the only way to increase living space.

■ Converting an existing garage is much cheaper than moving to a larger

Costs versus profit

The cost of a garage conversion can vary depending on a number of factors, including who you get to carry out the build and where you live in the UK. On average, however, employing a company to convert a single garage costs around £10,000–£15,000, while converting a double costs £15,000–£20,000. However, a good-quality garage conversion can add as much as a similar-sized extension, which is 10–15 per cent of the value of your home.

Example

If your house is worth £200,000, the maximum value you could add with a garage conversion is around £20,000–£30,000. Depending on what you want, a garage conversion can cost anything from £10,000 upwards, so there's definitely room for profit. However, there is a caveat to this. You need to work out how losing the garage will affect your outside space: if it leaves you with nothing but on-street parking or a tiny garden, you might lose any potential value gain.

home or building an extension from scratch.

■ Garages can be easily converted into a second reception room, a downstairs bedroom, a home office, or a playroom. The garage is often next to the kitchen, which makes it a prime candidate for turning into a large kitchen/diner without having to move drainage or plumbing.

■ A standard single garage is approximately 13.5 square metres, which is too small for most family cars, but plenty big enough for a comfortable, habitable room.

■ If you are lucky enough to have a double garage, you could have a 'part conversion', where the front or back of the garage might be retained for storage space, while the rest is converted into a usable room.

■ Many garage conversions don't need formal planning permission.

Do I have the right type of garage?

Almost any type of garage can be converted. A single garage is plenty big enough for a habitable room, while a double garage can easily be 'part converted', or changed into more than one room. A stand-alone garage (which isn't connected to the house)

can also be converted, but you might want to think carefully about what you'd use it for. A space away from the hustle and bustle of the house could make a good home office, but might not be popular as a bedroom or other living space. If your garage is not attached to your home, you might also have to apply for planning permission for change of use (see opposite).

Is it right for my house?

Here are some factors to consider if you are thinking of converting your garage into living accommodation.

■ Garage conversions can be difficult to get past planning if you live in an area with limited restricted parking. If you live in inner London or another busy city, you might have a battle on your hands.

■ Planners might also object to your plans if they include creating a new paved parking area to compensate for the loss of the garage. The planners will want to be reassured that you have adequate provision for rainwater drainage.

■ If your home is listed, you might not be able to convert the existing garage if it affects the character of the building.

■ Your home might contain a restrictive covenant that prevents you altering the appearance of the property or changing the use of your garage. Developers often put in these clauses to prevent people altering the look of their house while surrounding properties are still unsold. Check with your solicitor – you might be able to get the covenant lifted.

What about planning permission and Building Regulations?

Approximately 80 per cent of garage conversions don't require local authority planning permission. However, it's always essential to check with the local planning officer first. Occasionally, a garage conversion might require planning permission, often where permitted development rights have been removed. Whatever the case, you'll still have to comply with Building Regulations, particularly in relation to structural stability, glazing, insulation, ventilation, electrics and drainage.

DIY or get the professionals in?

The same rules apply to garage conversions as to house extensions. An advanced DIYer should be able to tackle many of the elements involved, from planning to management. If you want a very straightforward garage conversion, you can work out what space you need and draw up the plans yourself. However, it's important that you have a firm grasp of Building Regulations before you start.

As you're dealing with a pre-existing building, much of the hard work (foundations and walls) has already been done, but there are bits you shouldn't tackle yourself. You can fit the windows, but they'll need to be made by a FENSA-registered company or a contractor in a similar Competent Persons Scheme (see page 25). Otherwise, Building Control will need to come to your house and check that any new glazing complies with current energy-saving and thermal-efficiency standards. All domestic electrical work done nowadays, except very minor works, has to comply with Building Regulations. To ensure this you have either to employ someone who is registered with a Competent Persons Scheme, such as BRE, ELECSA, NICEIC or NAPIT, or else do the work yourself and pay for the local council's Building Control officer to check it. If you are going to do the building and structural work yourself, however, remember that it will be strictly monitored by Building Control.

If you live in a period property, or suspect you'll need planning permission for your garage conversion, it's advisable to consult an architect, who can guide you through the red tape, help you to get the most from the space, and project-manage if needed.

Builders will take on as little or as much of the project as you need. Many won't want to deal with the paperwork side of things, however, so it's worth clarifying who's going to be responsible for what.

Perhaps the best option is to employ a specialist garage conversion company. They can handle everything from Building Control to build quality, and will offer a guarantee on any work carried out. They'll also be much quicker than either a DIYer or a sole builder, as they'll be knowledgeable about the specific issues and problems involved. Lots of companies offer this service (see page 186 for more information).

an obvious improvement: central heating

It might seem like a no-brainer, but you'd be amazed how many homes don't have central heating. According to the last census, around one in 10 households still doesn't have central heating of any kind. In some parts of the UK, such as the Isles of Scilly, the figure is as high as four in 10 households. Cost and disruption are the two main reasons most people give for not installing central heating, but the reality is that it's one of the quickest ways to add value to your home. Why is it so important to house-hunters?

- Central heating is one of the principal must-haves on any house-buyer's wishlist. Homes without it get a chilly reaction from prospective buyers.
- Heating and hot-water systems consume far more energy than other household appliances. Central heating is the most cost-efficient way to heat your home compared with storage heaters, electric fan heaters and plug-in radiators.
- House-buyers expect to find every modern convenience already installed, even in a period property. A non-existent or dated heating system will knock thousands off the value of your home.
- Purchasers assume that getting central heating installed will be costly and disruptive, so do not want to do the work themselves.
- Houses that are permanently cold can suffer from damp and condensation. In the long run, these can lead to more serious structural problems, such as timber decay.

Costs versus profit

The figures speak for themselves. According to the Nationwide building society, adding central heating increases your home's value by an average of 7 per cent.

Example

The cost of installing a full central heating system is around £5000, so for the average £200,000 house you will add a heartwarming £14,000 in value. You may even qualify for a grant to help with the costs (see opposite). Even better, a new central heating system will also knock money off your energy bills.

Conversely, *not* having central heating seriously detracts from the value of your house, depending on where you live. In Scotland and the northwest, for example, having no central heating can knock off an alarming 12 per cent from your house value. In the warmer southwest, this figure is more like 5 per cent. See the table opposite to calculate your regional difference:

A new, efficient central heating system is likely to reduce your CO_2 emissions – something that will become increasingly important to home-buyers when (and if) Home Information Packs come into full force (see page 17).

Will I need planning permission?

You don't need planning permission for central heating unless your house is listed or in a Conservation Area. And even if your home *is* listed, it doesn't necessarily mean you can't have central heating – you might simply have to be more inventive about where you run the pipes and site the boiler.

What about Building Regulations?

There are very specific Building Regulations for central heating. The main rule is that boilers now have to meet

Region	Lost value without central heating
UK	6.8%
Scotland	12.1%
Yorkshire & Humberside	8.2%
London	6.4%
Southwest	4.6% SOURCE: NATIONWIDE

Central heating grants

You might be entitled to get financial help towards the cost of installing a new central heating system or upgrading an old one. The grants, which can be as generous as £4000, differ depending on where you live. The idea behind the scheme is to help vulnerable groups – such as those on a low income, people with disabilities, the elderly, pregnant women, and families with children – and you might need to be receiving certain types of benefit to qualify. However, the rules do change on an ongoing basis, and differ depending on where you live, so it's always worth contacting the organisation nearest to you and finding out if you qualify for help (see page 184).

a minimum level of efficiency. Other rules stipulate that any system now has to have a timer, a room thermostat, a hot-water tank thermostat and tank insulation. All new central heating systems have to be installed and tested by a competent person registered with an appropriate organisation (CORGI for gas, OFTEC for oil, and HETAS for solid fuel, for example). If you have an electric boiler fitted, make sure the wiring is completed by a registered tradesman.

What are my options?

If you live in a city, you can have your pick of central heating systems. Most urban areas have access to mains gas, but rural areas are often limited to bottled gas, oil tanks, or electric central heating. Here's a quick run-down of the pros and cons of each type.

Natural gas

Gas is the most common way to fuel your central heating system. It is piped directly into your home as you need it and, unlike some other fuels, doesn't

Annual fuel costs and carbon emissions for a typical semi-detached property

| | All fuel use | | | |
| | £ running cost | | kg carbon | |
	From	To	From	To
Electric peak heating	950	1780	1595	2915
Modern electric storage, automatic control	645	1180	1825	3615
Bulk LPG central heating (90%)	635	1065	1260	2245
Air source heat pump (250%)	575	990	1115	1885
Solid fuel boiler system (65%)	540	945	1980	3875
Wood pellet boiler system (65%)	495	850	525	675
Electric ground source heat pump (300%)	470	745	975	1570
Gas central heating – typical of stock (67%)	465	720	1335	2340
Electric ground source heat pump (320%)	455	720	955	1520
Oil central heating – A rated (90%)	405	645	1335	2405
Gas central heating – A rated (90%)	400	595	1075	1845

Percentages = seasonal efficiency of the system

need to be topped up. Many rural areas don't have mains natural gas, so you might have to choose a different option. Only suppliers licensed by Ofgem (Office of Gas and Electricity Markets) can sell you gas. You can obtain a list of gas suppliers from the Energy-watch website (see page 185). If you know you do not have access to mains gas but would like to get connected, find out more in the gas section of the National Grid website (see page 188). At the moment, piped gas is the cheapest form of energy.

Space and water heating only

| £ running cost | | kg carbon | |
From	To	From	To
750	1580	1195	2515
445	980	1425	3215
435	865	860	1845
375	790	715	1485
340	745	1580	3475
295	650	125	275
270	545	575	1170
265	520	935	1940
255	520	555	1120
205	445	935	2005
200	395	675	1445

Liquefied petroleum gas

LPG is a viable alternative when it is impossible to connect to a mains gas supply. Supplied to your home in bottles, LPG is a relatively expensive form of energy, and you will need a boiler that can be converted to use it. You also need to replace the bottles yourself when they run out.

Oil

This is another option if you cannot get access to mains gas. You will need to site a large oil tank on your premises, the location of which will be governed by Building Regulations. At the time of writing oil is slightly more expensive than gas, but still cheaper than LPG. The householder is responsible for refilling the oil tank.

Solid fuel

Central heating can be run on solid fuel, such as wood, anthracite pellets and coal, but these systems are somewhat dated because they use old technology, such as back boilers or kitchen ranges. However, as oil and gas supplies decline, solid fuel might become a more realistic alternative in the future. Meanwhile, if you want to renovate your house to sell, most buyers will expect a more conventional central heating system.

Electricity

Electric central heating is a relatively new phenomenon. Unlike storage heaters or other forms of electric heating, electric boilers can power conventional central heating systems with radiators, but have the benefit of being very compact and almost silent. At the time of writing the running costs of electric heating are more than oil or natural gas, but cheaper than LPG, and you can lower costs by making the most of economy tariffs. Electric boilers can also run off 'green' electricity – produced either by eco suppliers, such as Good Energy or Juice (see Green Energy, page 186), or by domestic renewables, such as wind turbines or photovoltaic panels. Manufacturers of modern electric boilers include Trianco, who make the 'Atzec' boiler, and Heatrae Sadia, who make the 'Amptec' boiler.

DIY or get the professionals in?

Building Regulations are very strict when it comes to installing new boilers, so it's probably best to leave this job to the professionals. As mentioned before, all new central heating systems have to be tested and passed by a tradesman who is registered with a Competent Persons Scheme (see page 184).

If you are an experienced DIYer, you might want to tackle the job of installing central heating yourself. Bear in mind that you will have to get your work inspected and approved by your local Building Control officer.

Top Tips

■ ■

Want to get the most from your heating? Here's how to warm your rooms without blowing your budget.

■ Consider putting designer radiators in key rooms, such as the bathroom and living room, and cheaper radiators in the rest of the house. Remember, you need to keep costs down without compromising the look of your home.

■ Think about the positioning of your radiators. Arrange them so they don't dominate a room, create an awkward space, or make a wall unusable.

■ Radiators don't have to be white. They are available in a range of colours, and in different finishes from chrome to satin polished.

■ Buy the correct size radiator for the room. If you haven't taken advice from a plumber or heating engineer, you can find a BTU (British Thermal Units) radiator size calculator on Heat & Plumb's website (see page 186).

■ If space is tight, use a thin, flat-panel radiator or a vertical design.

■ Consider buying Low Surface Temperature (LST) radiators if you have young children to prevent accidental burns.

■ If you have a period home, consider using traditional-style radiators, or sourcing refurbished originals from an architectural salvage yard.

■ ■

free improvements: no-cost ways to boost buyer appeal

It's all well and good talking about adding value to your home, but what if you don't have access to the kind of cash needed for big projects? Most people who want to improve the value, and therefore the sale price, of their house can take plenty of positive steps without resorting to big bucks. Equally, if you've spent your hard-earned money on significant home improvements, such as a new kitchen or a loft conversion, you certainly don't want the rest of the house to let you down.

At the end of the day your home is a commodity. It's worth only what someone is prepared to pay for it and, as such, will fetch a good price only if it's well presented. If you're thinking of getting your home revalued, or putting it up for sale, how can you improve its saleability without having to spend a penny?

Have a good clear-out

Don't be tempted to shove all your unwanted gear into the nearest cupboard or stuff the garage to the gills. You need to create the illusion that you have more space than you know what to do with. Removing clutter also makes it easier for buyers to imagine their own belongings in a room. Be ruthless: recycle, reduce and reuse. Send your unwanted items off to the charity shop or the tip. What you can't bear to throw away can perhaps be temporarily housed with a helpful relative. The net result is that your home will feel much, much bigger.

Keep on top of the tidying

How many of us have done a mad spring-clean before a house sale and then let the mess slowly build up again? It's a pain to have to keep your house in tip-top 'show home' condition, but nothing kills a house sale

more quickly than a sink full of dirty dishes. Keep on top of the cleaning as long as your house is on the market. Pay particular attention to bathrooms and kitchens – these should be spotless.

Banish bad smells

The smallest details can deter a buyer from making an offer. Smells are particularly evocative and can quickly change the mind of a prospective purchaser. Get rid of all traces of smoke, cooking, strong cleaning products and whiffy pets. Avoid air fresheners – they make it look like you're trying to mask something.

Pack off the pooch

Forget trying to disguise the dog smell – send your pooch packing. You might dote on your doggie, but not all prospective purchasers are animal lovers. Can Granny take care of Fido for a fortnight? If so, jump at the opportunity. The same goes for all other furry and feathered friends.

Go one further

Why stop at offloading the pets? An empty house is much easier to sell. Is there anywhere the family can crash while the viewings take place? Estate agents prefer you not to be there when they're showing people around. Think about it from the buyers' perspective – they're planning to spend a lot of money and need to get the measure of your house. If your family is mooching about, buyers will feel inhibited and rush the viewing, making it much less likely that they'll make an offer.

Kerbside appeal

It's a truism, but there's no denying that most buyers will have decided whether they like your home in the first 15 seconds. Drive or walk up to your house and see how it looks from the street. Clean the windows and front door. Polish the door furniture and house plate. Clear the gutters. Hide the bins. Tidy the drive and front garden. Put the car in the garage. Make sure any exterior lights are working, and leave them on during the evening – lots of buyers do an initial drive-by to see how your house looks.

Look at it through fresh eyes

Ask a trusted friend or the estate agent to do a mock viewing. If you've lived in the house for any length of time, you'll have long stopped noticing the building's shortcomings. Ask them to be truthful about the first impression your home makes: is there anything they would change or make a feature of? Be prepared for some uncomfortable home truths.

Let your estate agent do her job

The key to getting a house sold quickly is to have a good working relationship with your agent. Resist showing people around yourself. Buyers prefer estate agents to show them around a property – it's more professional, less intrusive, and you tend to get more honest feedback from buyers about the strengths and weaknesses of the house. It also avoids the vendor having to answer awkward questions about why they're selling.

Time the viewings right

Timing is everything when it comes to showing buyers around a property. If you live near a school, avoid viewings in the early morning and mid-afternoon when it's often noisy and difficult to park. The same goes for houses next to main roads and busy venues, such as restaurants and pubs. Choose a time when the house isn't compromised by fixed factors outside your control.

Timing also matters in terms of *when* you put your property on the market. The best times for selling are spring and autumn; the market slows down during late summer and over Christmas, although there tends to be a brief boost around New Year. If you can hold on until a more buoyant time of the year, do. If a property is sold while the market is strong, it's much more likely to attract a good price.

Be a good neighbour

Can your relationship with the neighbours affect your house value? Yes! Bad-tempered, noisy or difficult neighbours can certainly make your home a trickier place to sell. If you've had any official disputes with your neighbours, they will have to be declared during the conveyancing process, and might put prospective purchasers off completing the sale. Fostering a good relationship with the people on your street will not only make life infinitely more pleasurable, but will also reap its own rewards. As mentioned in the Introduction (page 13), when communities are encouraged to club together and improve their surroundings, they see a significant increase in the value of their homes. Setting up a voluntary community scheme, creating a Neighbourhood Watch group, campaigning for better council facilities, or even entering your neighbourhood for the

Britain in Bloom competition are all great ways to improve neighbour relations and boost your home's value in the process.

Useful contacts

Telephone numbers are included wherever available, but please note that some of the following organisations can be contacted only online.

APHC – Association of Plumbing and Heating Contractors
024 7647 0626
www.aphc.co.uk
Oversees a Competent Persons Scheme relating to heating and plumbing work.

Armitage Shanks Ltd
01543 490253
www.armitage-shanks.co.uk
Bathroom manufacturer.

Auro Paints
01452 772020
www.auro.co.uk
Manufactures natural paints and wood finishes.

B&Q
www.diy.co.uk
DIY store and information.

Georgina Barrow
01451 861040
www.naturalpaints.org.uk
Produces traditional water-based paints.

Basement Information Centre
01276 33155
www.basements.org.uk
Specialist contractors for drainage, tunnelling, waterproofing, underpinning and finishing work on basement conversions.

Bat Conservation Trust
0845 1300 228
www.bats.org.uk
Offers advice to householders and builders on dealing with bats.

Bathstore
08000 23 23 23
www.bathstore.com
The UK's largest bathroom retailer.

BBC Homes
www.bbc.co.uk/homes
Free home improvement advice.

BESCA – Building Engineering Services Competence Accreditation
www.besca.org.uk
Oversees a Competent Persons Scheme relating to heating, ventilation and plumbing.

Big in Bathrooms
www.biginbathrooms.co.uk
Online bathroom store with planning service.

Bricks and Brass
020 8290 1488
www.bricksandbrass.co.uk
Has a useful database on the architecture, design and history of domestic buildings. Includes advice on period house maintenance.

British Gas
0845 955 5200
www.britishgas.co.uk
Offers advice and information about saving energy.

British Standards Institution
020 8290 1488
www.bsi-global.com
Oversees several Competent Persons Schemes, including those for door and window fitters.

Building Conservation Directory
www.buildingconservation.com
An online list of suppliers, products and services related to conservation. Great if you need to find tradesmen who know about restoration issues.

Building Control
www.labc.uk.com
National organisation representing Building Control departments in England, Wales and Northern Ireland, with information for householders.

Building Estimates
www.Estimators-Online.com
Offers estimates for one- and two-storey extensions.

Central Heating Grants
Central Heating Programme (Scotland)
0800 316 1653
www.scotland.gov.uk

Home Energy Efficiency Scheme (Wales)
0800 316 2815
www.heeswales.co.uk

Warm Deal (Scotland)
0800 316 6009
www.chwdp-scottishexecutive.co.uk/central/central.php

Warm Front (England)
0800 316 2805
www.warmfrontgrants.co.uk

Warm Homes Scheme (N. Ireland)
0800 181 667
www.eaga.com/government_contracts/warmerhomes.htm

Channel 4 Homes
www.Channel4.com/Homes
Free home improvement advice.

Communities and Local Government
020 7944 4400
www.communities.gov.uk
Government department responsible for housing, local government, regeneration, planning and urban and regional issues.

Community Matters
020 7226 0189
www.communitymatters.org.uk
Charitable federation for community associations. Good publications on setting up and running community organisations and buildings.

Competent Persons Schemes
www.communities.gov.uk/planning andbuilding
Government website listing numerous approved schemes.

Conservation Register
020 7721 8246
www.conservationregister.com
Holds detailed information on conservation/restoration experts across the UK and Ireland.

CORGI – Confederation for the Registration of Gas Installers
0800 915 0485
www.trustcorgi.com
Organisation of approved gas installers.

DIY Doctor
www.diydoctor.org.uk
Free online advice and guidance on self-build and DIY.

DIY Fixit
www.diyfixit.co.uk
Free online advice and guidance on DIY home improvements.

Dry Stone Walling Association
01539 567953
www.dswa.org.uk
Promotes the highest standards of craftsmanship and lists certificated wallers.

Dulux
020 8290 1488
www.dulux.co.uk
Offers inspiration, product advice and a paint calculator.

Earthborn Paints
01928 734171
www.earthbornpaints.co.uk
Produces high-quality paints that are free of VOCs.

Ecos Organic Paints
01524 852371
www.ecospaints.com
Manufactures natural, solvent-free paints.

Energy Saving Trust
0800 512 012
www.energysavingtrust.org.uk
Advice on eco-friendly home improvements.

Energywatch
08459 06 07 08
www.energywatch.org.uk
Offers a list of gas suppliers in the UK.

Environment Agency
08708 506 506
www.environment-agency.gov.uk
Information about environmental risks, such as flooding, landfills, radon and air pollution in your area.

Estimators Online
www.Estimators-Online.com
For a small fee, offers a good approximation of the cost of any proposed extension.

Farrow & Ball
01202 876141
www.farrow-ball.com
Manufacturers of traditional paints and wallpapers.

Federation of Master Builders
0800 015 2522
www.findabuilder.co.uk
Organisation that lists approved builders. Also has a free contract that you can download and use for any building project.

FENSA – Fenestration Self-Assessment Scheme
0870 780 2028
www.fensa.org.uk
Oversees a Competent Persons Scheme that lists approved glazing contractors.

Find a Builder
see Federation of Master Builders

Focus DIY
0800 436 436
www.focusdiy.co.uk
DIY store and information.

Forest Stewardship Council
www.fsc.org
An accreditation scheme for ethically sourced timber.

Garage Conversions
www.garageconversion.com
www.GarageConversionExperts.com
www.garageconversionsuk.co.uk
www.space-solutions.co.uk
www.thegarageconversioncompany.co.uk
www.vogue-garage-conversion.co.uk

Garage Plans
www.garageplans.co.uk
Offers a selection of standard garage plans, and can draw up custom-designed garages.

Geffrye Museum
020 7739 9893
www.geffrye-museum.org.uk
Inspiration for anyone thinking of restoring an historic interior.

Glass and Glazing Federation
0870 042 4255
www.ggf.co.uk
Offers a guide to choosing the right conservatory.

Green Energy Helpline
0800 634 16 06
www.green.energyhelpline.com
CO_2 footprint and price comparison service that provides customers with free advice on their best green energy deal.

Guild of Architectural Ironmongers
020 7790 3431
www.gai.org.uk
Seeks to promote and maintain standards within the industry; also lists those who adhere to its code of practice.

Guild of Master Craftsmen
01273 478449
www.guildmc.com
Has a nationwide register of master craftsmen, including builders, kitchen fitters, carpenters, electricians, furniture-makers, gardeners, glaziers, plumbers, roofers and woodworkers.

Harvey Jones
0800 389 6938
www.harveyjones.com
Specialists in handmade kitchens.

Heat & Plumb
www.heatandplumb.com
Heating and plumbing supplies, plus expert advice.

Heatrae Sadia
01603 420100
www.electroheatplc.co.uk
Makers of the electric Amptec boiler.

HETAS – Heating Equipment Testing and Approval Scheme
0845 634 5626
www.hetas.co.uk
Government-recognised body that approves solid-fuel domestic heating appliances, fuels and services.

Homebase
0845 077 8888
www.homebase.co.uk
DIY store and information.

Home Information Packs (HIPs)
www.homeinformationpacks.gov.uk
Government website providing information about the new HIPs scheme.

House Extension Online
www.house-extension.co.uk
Internet guide to house extensions.

HVCA – Heating & Ventilation Contractors' Association
020 7313 4900
www.hvca.org.uk
Oversees a Competent Persons Scheme relating to heating, ventilating and air-conditioning.

Hydraulic Parking Systems
www.doubleparking.co.uk
www.intergarage3000gb.com
www.totalparkingsolutions.co.uk

Ideal Standard
0800 590 311
www.ideal-standard.co.uk
Bathroom manufacturer.

IKEA
0845 358 3363
www.ikea.com
Wide range of home furnishings, including kitchens and storage solutions.

Independent Financial Advisers
www.searchifa.co.uk
www.ifa-guide.co.uk
www.unbiased.co.uk

International Paints
08447 709 444
www.international-paints.co.uk
Suppliers of specialist paints, including anti-condensation paint.

KBSA – Kitchen Bathroom Bedroom Specialists Association
01905 621787
www.kbsa.co.uk
Free planning, design and buying advice.

Law Society
020 7242 1222
www.lawsociety.org.uk
Information on crucial aspects of property law.

Leasehold Advisory Service
020 7374 5380
www.lease-advice.org
Offers free advice on the law affecting residential long leasehold property and commonhold.

Listed Property Owners Club
01795 844939
www.lpoc.co.uk
A good source of information and
support for anyone who owns a listed
building.

Magnet
0845 123 6789
www.magnet.co.uk
Kitchen suppliers.

MFI
0800 023 4457
www.mfi.co.uk
The UK's leading retailer of fitted kitchens, bathrooms and bedrooms.

Money Supermarket
www.moneysupermarket.com
Price comparison website, including
mortgages, credit cards, and personal
and home improvement loans.

NAPIT – National Association of Professional Inspectors and Testers
0870 4441392
www.napit.org.uk
Oversees a Competent Persons Scheme
relating to heating, plumbing and ventilation.

National Association of Estate Agents
01926 496800
www.naea.co.uk
Find a reputable estate agent near you.

National Conservatory Advisory Service
0870 770 6606
www.nrwas.org
Advice on different ways of improving,
building or extending your home.

National Federation of Roofing Contractors
020 7436 0387
www.nfrc.co.uk
Find a qualified roofer near you.

National Grid
0845 605 6677
www.nationalgrid.com
Information on getting connected to
national electricity and gas supplies.

National Home Improvement Council
020 7448 3853
www.nhic.org.uk
Represents companies and organisations
that work in the home improvement
sector.

NICEIC – National Institute of Certification of Construction (Electrical Installations)
0870 013 0382
www.niceic.org.uk
Oversees a Competent Persons Scheme
relating to electrical contractors.

npower
www.npower.com
Electricity supplier that also offers advice
and information about green energy.

Nutshell Paints
01392 823760
www.nutshellpaints.co.uk
Produces solvent-free, biodegradable paints.

Ofgem – Office of Gas and Electricity Markets
0845 906 0708
www.ofgem.gov.uk
Regulates gas and electricity suppliers.

OFTEC – Oil Firing Technical Association
0845 65 85 080
www.oftec.org.uk
Oversees a Competent Persons Scheme relating to oil installers.

Paint Quality Institute
www.paintquality.co.uk
Information on everything to do with paint, including a quantity calculator.

Period Features
01538 372202
www.periodfeatures.net
Excellent shop (in Leek, Staffordshire) and online store, selling hardware, paints and accessories for period homes and gardens.

Period Property UK
www.periodproperty.co.uk
Helpful information on period properties, their character and maintenance, plus a directory of craftsmen and professionals.

Planning Inspectorate
0117 372 6372 (England);
029 2082 3866 (Wales)
www.planning-inspectorate.gov.uk
Details of how to appeal against a refusal of planning permission.

Planning Portal
www.planningportal.gov.uk
Free government planning advice.

Plumb World
www.plumbworld.co.uk
The UK's largest online retailer of bathrooms.

Property Forecasts
www.propertyforecasts.co.uk
Provides 3–5-year forecasts of house prices for most postcode sectors and districts in England and Wales.

Repair Products
020 8648 3866
www.repairproducts.co.uk
Source of repair kits for laminate work surfaces.

RIBA – Royal Institute of British Architects
020 7307 3700
www.architecture.com
Has a list of its 28,000 members and offers a tailored search to find an architect to suit your needs.

Richmond Oak Bespoke Conservatories
01908 511434
www.oakconservatories.co.uk
Designs and builds individually tailored conservatories.

Royal Institution of Chartered Surveyors
0870 333 1600
www.rics.org
Has a register of RICS-qualified chartered surveyors.

Royal Town Planning Institute
020 7960 5663
www.rtpiconsultants.co.uk
Has a register that will help you to find a planning consultant near you.

Salvo
www.salvo.co.uk
The UK's most comprehensive salvage website.

Saniflo
0800 072 8822
www.saniflo.co.uk
Manufacturer of pumping systems, including macerating toilet pumps.

Society for the Protection of Ancient Buildings
020 7377 1644
www.spab.org.uk
Offers advice about restoring period properties.

Trianco
0114 257 2300
www.trianco.co.uk
Makers of the electric Atzec boiler.

Up My Street
www.upmystreet.com
Specific information about your post-code, including average house prices, housing trends, demographics, local schools and crime rates.

Wickes
0800 106068
www.wickes.co.uk
DIY store and information.

Index
Italic numbers indicate illustrations.